Secret History

Secret History

A Translation of
Vor Tids Muhamed

by

John Ahmanson

**Translated
by**

Gleason L. Archer

MOODY PRESS
CHICAGO

**Library of Congress Cataloging in Publica-
tion Data**

Ahmanson, John.
  Secret history.

  1. Mormon Church—Controversial litera-
ture. 2. Church of Jesus Christ of Latter-Day
Saints—Controversial literature. 3. Ahman-
son, John. 4. Ex-church members—Mormon
Church—Biography. 5. Ex-church mem-
bers—Church of Jesus Christ of Latter-Day
Saints—Biography.
  I. Title.
BX 8645.A313 1984   289.3   84-621
ISBN: 0-8024-0277-1

1 2 3 4 5 6 7 Printing/AF/Year 89 88 87 86 85 84

Printed in the United States of America

Contents

Translator's Preface

It was a real privilege for me to be involved in the translation of this remarkable work, even though it came to me in a totally unexpected manner. I first became aware of the book when William Welty, a former student of mine at Trinity Evangelical Divinity School, sent me a photocopy of the first few pages, published in the old-fashioned Gothic font common to all of the Scandinavian languages prior to World War I. Perhaps it was because of this format that local Danes in Southern California had been unable to do much with it. And so it ultimately devolved upon me to undertake the translation myself, at the behest of the Fieldstead Institute. Although I was already involved in the production of other works that were being readied for publication, I consented to crowd this project into a busy summer schedule in 1981. After I had got deeply into Mr. Ahmanson's narrative, I realized that I was looking at the most effective and devastating exposé of Mormonism that I had ever seen.

The effectiveness of *Vor Tids Muhamed* (as the title reads in Danish) lies principally in its eyewitness testimony furnished by a very intelligent and perceptive man who had first become a committed disciple of the Mormon faith and who later by personal experience became aware that it was not really based upon the teaching of the Bible as understood and interpreted by the historic Christian church. Although Joseph Smith was already dead by the time of Ahmanson's conversion, he nevertheless came to know Brigham Young very well in Salt Lake City in the 1850s. His reports of what was said and done in the Utah Territory in that period result in large measure from his eyewitness observation, or from conversation with others who were participants in the events narrated. This gives to his little book the character of a historic document, especially in view of the fact that it was published before the death of Brigham Young himself. Although much of it may be classed as hearsay evidence, the early date of its composition serves to enhance its credibility and trustworthiness in a very significant way.

It is only to be regretted that this potent document of analysis and solemn warning was not earlier put into English and made available to the general public. Had it been produced a century ago, it would unquestionably have dissuaded multitudes of families approached by the ever-diligent Mormon missionaries all across America from being taken in by this dangerous counterfeit of the historic Christian faith. Yet even at this late date, over a century after its first publication in Danish, it may still prove very helpful in warning prospective converts of the serious distortions of Christ's gospel and of historical reality that are involved in subscribing to the teachings of the Latter-Day Saints. It is even possible that those who have been reared in that religion may be moved to re-examine and repudiate the antiscriptural viewpoints and doctrines that characterize the Mormon faith. A fair and honest examination of the data contained in this little book make any other response almost impossible to justify in the face of such overwhelming evidence.

GLEASON L. ARCHER

Introduction to This Translation

This volume, which has been retitled *Secret History: An Eyewitness Account of the Rise of Mormonism*, is essentially an English translation of a Danish-language work by John Ahmanson that first appeared in 1876. Originally entitled *Vor Tids Muhamed* ("A Mohammed of Our Time"), Mr. Ahmanson's book was published at the press of the Danish Pioneer in Omaha, Nebraska.

The Fieldstead Institute undertook the responsibility for its translation almost by accident. A microfilm print (of rather poor quality) of the original Danish publication was sent to the Institute offices as part of the archives of the Ahmanson family, with a directive to have the book translated into English for the purpose of scholarly study. The Fieldstead Institute retained the services of Dr. Gleason L. Archer, professor of Old Testament and Semitic languages, Trinity Evangelical Divinity School, Deerfield, Illinois, for the translation work. A respected linguist, Dr. Archer informed the Institute of what he called the "historic importance" of the work.

Subject Matter

Secret History is a study of the origins and emergence into the mainstream of American religious life of the Church of Jesus Christ of Latter-day Saints—the Mormons. As described in the text, the author was a convert to Mormonism. He emigrated to Utah from his native Denmark in 1856, six years after his conversion. *Secret History* thus becomes an eyewitness chronicle of some of the early and formative years of Mormon history, told from the vantage point of an early convert who knew Brigham Young personally and who subsequently left the Mormon Church.

Ahmanson's book concludes with a commentary on the history of the court trial surrounding the infamous "Mountain Meadows Massacre" of 1857. Internal textual evidence (see the last few pages of the final chapter) suggests the possibility that the book was hastily published about the time of the trial, which commenced nearly two decades after the incidents that are so graphically portrayed in Ahmanson's memoirs. For a fascinating study of another aspect of Mr. Ahmanson's dealings with the Mormons, see the Spring 1983 issue of *Nebraska History*, which contains an article entitled "John Ahmanson vs. Brigham Young: A Nebraska Legal Controversy, 1859-1861."

The Original Book

The Fieldstead Institute has been able to locate only three copies of the original publication. One is on closed reserve in the Rollins Collection, Western Americana Division, of the Library of Princeton University, Princeton, New Jersey. A second copy is registered in the Library of Congress, Washington, D.C. The work is listed in *The National Union Catalog of Pre-1956 Imprints, Volume V* (page 848, #NA010452). Published in Danish, the book is set in a Gothic type face (similar to the German *Fraktur*). The original copy made available to the Institute was printed on white paper, measuring 17.0 cm × 10.7 cm, with a purple title page. One hundred seventy pages long, the rebound copy that the Institute used for translation weighed 5.2 ounces and had a hardbound cover measuring 18.3 cm × 15.6 cm. The book's thickness is 1.0 cm.

ABOUT THE PRESENT WORK

John Ahmanson's original work is now in the public domain. This English translation, however, has been produced by the Fieldstead Institute, which is solely responsible for the accuracy of the translation. After an initial draft of the translation was made by Dr. Archer, the work was submitted for verification of its accuracy to a native of Denmark, who at the time of this project was living in the United States, undertaking postgraduate studies at Trinity Evangelical Divinity School.

The reader will note that this translation is equipped with a complete textual apparatus. The first register contains the original author's footnotes to his book; they were a part of the 1876 edition. Those original author footnotes are indicated in the main body of the text by superscript lowercase letters ([a, b, c,] etc.).

The second register of the textual apparatus was not part of the original publication. It consists of a running historical commentary and bibliography on Mr. Ahmanson's original narrative. Chris Alex Vlachos served as a consulting research editor for the assembly of this register. A resident of Provo, Utah, Mr. Vlachos utilized the excellent resources available in the library of Brigham Young University for research into both the accuracies and inaccuracies of the allegations made by Ahmanson. Several respected experts on Mormon history and theology, such as Dr. Wesley P. Walters, Jerald and Sandra Tanner, and Dr. Walter Martin, were also consulted. The historical observations compiled by Mr. Vlachos are indicated in the body of the text by superscript Arabic numerals.

In addition, to facilitate scholarly research and discussion among interested students of Mormon history, the Fieldstead Institute has added translator notes by Dr. Archer, along with a few selected notations by the editor of this edition, Mr. William Welty. Those comments are intended mainly to clarify certain ambiguities that sprang up in the course of the actual translation and editing processes themselves. Those translator and editor comments are indicated in the main body of the text by a superscript asterisk (*). Each asterisk will be accompanied by its corresponding note at the right-hand margin of the page.

To facilitate comparisons between the Fieldstead Institute translation and the original Danish work, we have endeavored to indicate page divisions in the 1876 edition. Those page divisions are marked by brackets, followed immediately by the new page number (e.g., [3]). Note that the original text of *Vor Tids Mohamed* began on page **3**.

Preface to the Original Edition

Although much has been said and written concerning Mormonism, its origin, teachings, strategy, and so forth, yet there is very little that has been set forth in Danish. What little there is that has been imparted has consisted essentially of translation from foreign authors, or else of descriptions based upon individual observations and experiences during a sojourn of brief or lengthier duration among the Mormons in Utah. The purpose of this present little essay is to give to the Danish public a condensed historical account of the origin and spread of Mormonism, and also to unveil the mysterious and deceptive system on which it is based, not only for its genesis but also for its almost unbelievable mysteries and crimes to which it has continually resorted in order to preserve its power and influence.

As I thus render an unreserved account and set forth the "endowment mysteries" of Mormonism and some of its best known crimes of bloodshed in Utah, it is nevertheless by no means my purpose to accuse all those who call themselves Mormons as being partakers of, or involved in, such crimes as these. On the contrary it appears from the judicial hearings held in Utah that the crimes were generally perpetrated in secret and as much as possible without the knowledge of the people themselves. It is sufficient that we know that the heads and leaders of the Church in most cases have formulated the plans and perpetrated the crimes, and that the Church [p.4] teaches and sanctions them. There are probably thousands of our compatriots living in Utah who because of the language factor alone are not only ignorant about Mormonism and its history in general, but also about the unnatural and criminal obligations which they have entered into in "the Endowment House." In the belief that the truth, the naked and unreserved truth—even though it be bitter and disappointing for many—is the only sure means of leading these misguided but honest and upright people out of the shameful slavery of Mormonism, and back to the kind and humanitarian teaching of Christ (and possibly rescue others also from being led astray by this brazen and clever deception)—this is another and no less important a purpose for the publication of this book.

I know full well that Mormonism is no poetic or interesting theme to treat of; nor is it for that reason a matter of my personal inclination, but rather through a sense of duty, after so many years of silence, that I am compelled to expose the false teachings and crimes of Mormonism—according to irrefutable historical information that Brigham's emissaries would never be in a position to refute. In America (the cradle of Mormonism) and England the Mormon propaganda has long since almost entirely ceased, and it now scarcely exists (except in our Scandinavian countries) in a single place anymore. Yet in them it apparently still continues on. May we not venture to hope that these also will follow the example of their great and enlightened neighbors?

Since I am not, nor make any claim to be, an author in the proper meaning of the term, my book will undoubtedly appear to suffer from many drawbacks and defects; but in this regard I hope that my enlightened and gracious readers will show indulgence and accept my good intentions in lieu of my imperfect performance.

JOHN AHMANSON
OMAHA, JULY 1876

1 The Introduction of Mormonism into Denmark

The general freedom which the constitution of 1849 had conferred upon the Danish people furnished support, as is well known, to a spiritual awakening and a strong inner life which expressed itself in many ways. In spite of the long-lasting and burdensome war (1848-50), or perhaps precisely because of it, patriotism mounted higher than ever in the heart of the people. It was not individual patriots but the entire Danish nation that mourned over the affair of Skjaertorsdag and rejoiced at the Battle of Fredericia. The mood of the time seems to have taken on a special receptivity toward the impact of events which for the most part would otherwise have been without interest. In the religious sphere as well, an unusual stir held sway at that time, especially among the various sects whose adherents had formerly suffered persecution and suppression.

Under these favorable circumstances a hitherto unknown sect in Denmark suddenly made its appearance, boldly calling itself "The Church of Jesus Christ of the Latter Day Saints"[1]—but later on after its progress began

---

1. Originally, the Mormon church was named "The Church of Christ" (see *Doctrine and Covenants*, 20:1, current *Doctrine and Covenants* copyright page, or the *Book of Commandments*, 1833 edition). On May 3, 1834, the name was changed to the "Church of the Latter-day Saints" (see *Documentary History of the Church* (Salt Lake City: Deseret, 1951), 2:63. On April 26, 1838, it was changed to the "Church of Jesus Christ of Latter-day Saints" (see *Doctrine and Covenants*, 115:3-4).

to arouse attention, an article appearing in Faedrelandet*
informed the laity that the common name of the sect was
"Mormons"!

In America this new gospel had already been proclaimed for many years, and four missionaries [p. 6] were
sent from there and who came to Copenhagen in the summer of 1850. They consisted of two Americans, Erastus
Snow and G. B. Dykes, and one Dane named B. O. Hansen,[2] and finally a certain Swede.[3] Snow, who was one of
the twelve apostles of New Zion, was the leader of the
mission, while Hansen was their interpreter and secretary.

This author at that time occasionally attended a Baptist
Church which held services in the Hotel Scandinavia on
the corner of King Street and King's New Market. The
pastor, a certain Mr. Mønster, gave the impression of being
to all appearances a highly gifted man, and likewise the
church seemed in regard to Christianity to be in a flourishing condition. But remarkably enough the new sect won
its very first proselytes in Denmark among these Baptists.

One Sunday we saw the above-mentioned four strangers
enter the meeting-hall and sit down near the doorway. No
one paid any further attention to them or had any slightest
inkling as yet regarding their intentions. But the sober,
almost deferential piety which they showed, in common
with all Americans, at religious services, gave rise to a
favorable opinion of them. They came frequently, made
the acquaintance of the pastor and many members of the
congregation, and gained admission to their homes, and
then began little by little to speak about their mission, and
they preached their new gospel. Their narrations concerning the miraculous call of the new prophet and his revelations naturally awakened great interest and discussion,
and so Pastor Mønster proceeded to an investigation of the
matter. But Apostle Snow handled him so cleverly that he
himself, without actually becoming a Mormon, seemed for
a time to be altogether drawn in that direction and convinced of the divine calling of the new prophet. His sermons became larded up with the Old Testament prophets

---

2. Peter O. Hansen; see *Comprehensive History of the Church* (Salt Lake
   City: Deseret, 1930), 3:390.
3. This seems to have been John Forsgren; see *Comprehensive History of
   the Church*, 3:390.

and with expositions of passages from John's Revelation, and of original previsions of great coming events, inasmuch as "The fullness of time was at hand," etc., etc. And this naturally served to make the congregation uneasy and to prepare the way still more for the Mormons. These latter had devised a long series of arguments in favor [p. 7] of this doctrine, supported by cleverly manipulated fragments of the Bible and from history. The line of argument went about as follows: The true Christian church died out under the persecutions of the first centuries; the Roman church which later assumed the spiritual sovereignty in Christendom and thereby became the mother of all the later churches and sects, could not of course have possessed any "apostolic succession" or spiritual authority that descended directly from the first apostolic church. On the contrary, this was the "Harlot" which was spoken of in Revelation 17:3-6.[4] They referred to the present conflicts, schisms, sects and parties within Christendom, and they asked triumphantly whether this could be that Church which was supposed to have "one faith, one baptism, one God the Father of all?"

Inasmuch as no such priesthood can be shown to stem directly from the apostles, and it stands written that "no one takes this honor to himself, unless he has been called thereto by God, as Aaron was," where should the authority come from except by a new direct revelation from heaven? But that had now taken place! God had once again visited the earth and raised up a prophet just as in the old days and called him and proclaimed to him "the everlasting Gospel (Revelation 14:6) for all families, tribes, language groups and nations." The Church of Christ was once again established upon the earth, and in possession of all the spiritual gifts and blessings which it had at "the beginning." "The scattered sheep of Israel" would again be gathered together, so that it would become "one flock and one Shepherd." As a further proof of the genuineness of this doctrine

4. Mormon apostle Orson Pratt wrote that all churches other than the LDS church were destitute of all authority to administer the sacraments: "But who in this generation have authority to baptize? None but those who have received authority in the Church of Jesus Christ of Latter-day Saints: all other churches are entirely destitute of all authority from God . . . Both Catholics and Protestants are nothing less than the 'whore of Babylon'. . . ." (*The Seer*, Washington ed., p. 255).

and faith, reference was made to the sufferings and persecutions which their church had already sustained in America, where the prophet Joseph Smith, his brother Hyrum,
and many of the "saints" had sealed the doctrine with their
blood and suffered martyrdom.[5]

The teachings of the missionaries found a fruitful soil
among the Baptists. There was even talk of entire congregations going over to Mormonism, with Pastor Mønster at
their head. It did not actually go that far, but many did
convert to the doctrine of the new apostle, and a new
denomination was speedily organized under the name
[p. 8] of "The Church of Jesus Christ of the Latter Day
Saints."* The enthusiasm of these proselyters was unbounded, because it truly seemed like the fire that animat-
ed the first Christians had returned once again in their
association. Those who were newly baptized were blessed
by the laying on of hands in order that they might receive
"the gift of the Holy Spirit" in connection with the prophetic declaration: "And thou shalt live and see Christ
coming again to earth to reign with all His saints."[a6] Parents were to bring forth their little children so that they
may receive similar blessings themselves, etc.

*The Dan-
ish reads
"Jesu
Kristi
Kirtes
sidste
Dages
Hellige."
—Trans.

I, the author, did not remain untouched by this general
movement; at first I tried for a long time sincerely to com-
bat their proofs and arguments, but these men possessed
an extraordinary knowledge of the Bible and understood
very well how to make use of it.—Soon I was convinced in
heart concerning the biblical truth of the teaching, but my
mind contended for a long time still against the unheard-of
and unbelievable elements in the whole matter. Could not

---

a. Joseph Smith says in his autobiography: "I once prayed to God very
earnestly that I might get to know the time of the coming of the Son
of Man, and I heard a voice that said, 'My son Joseph, if thou livest
to become eighty-five years old, thou shalt see the face of the Son of
Man; therefore let this be sufficient and do not trouble Me about
this matter.' " Joseph Smith was born in 1805, and so this great
event was to take place in 1890.

---

5. "Martyrdom." According to contemporary witnesses Joseph Smith
killed two men and wounded a third in the gun battle that ended his
life in the Carthage jail; see *Documentary History of the Church*, 6:617-
18; 7:100-103.

6. For an indepth treatment of prophecies relating to Christ's second
coming see *Mormonism: Shadow or Reality?* (Salt Lake City: Utah
Lighthouse Ministry, 1982), pp. 187-88.

the missionaries be either deceived or deceivers of others?

It was really not reasonable to take them to be victims of deception, for their knowledge and utterance concerning the new teaching was too decisive and circumstantial for that. For several years they had personally known and kept company with Joseph Smith. They were all far from religious fanaticism; on the contrary their activities were practical their goals were near at hand [sic]. Besides, all of these events to which they gave testimony had taken place in an enlightened Christian country. Even the prophet himself with his youth and meager education seemed hardly to have been suited to lead such enlightened and thoughtful people away from the light.

Even more unreasonable did it seem to me to take them as deceivers, for what would their purpose be in that? [p. 9] They had forsaken their house and home, their wife and children in order to devote themselves to foreign and remote portions of the earth and proclaim the gospel to their fellow men without any kind of remuneration. Their life and daily conduct seemed to conform very closely to the doctrine they preached.

Such reflections as these necessarily had to impel me eventually, through many trials and temptations, to an unavoidable "either . . . or"—that is, either to accept the new teaching or to give up my faith in the Bible as God's word.—I chose the former. Therefore I got baptized and taken into the "resurrected Christian Church." This took place at the close of 1850.

That which took place in Copenhagen in regard to the introduction of Mormonism was soon afterwards repeated in Aalborg, where there was also a large Baptist church. G. P. Dykes was sent there, and he was moreover the one of the missionaries who possessed the most spiritual training combined with an uncommonly prepossessing and well-mannered behavior.[b]

Thereupon in 1851 Mormonism was exported to Norway by a Captain Swen Larsen, who sailed between Aalborg and the East Riis Islands. In the aforementioned city he was converted and baptized. The "Book of Mormon," which P. D. Hansen had already translated into Danish,

---

b. After his return to Utah he abandoned Mormonism.

had now been printed and published along with "Book of the Covenants,"[7] but since the contents of these books by no means lived up to the expectations which had been conceived of them as a consequence of their marvelous origin, the Bible continued still to be their infallible "touchstone" and weapon of their faith, both for attack and for defense. But by looking over the Mormon scriptures, insofar as they had already appeared in Danish, I soon found out that we had by this time barely taken hold of the introductory teachings; for the Apostles had imparted only "a little here and a little there," since they presumably believed that we were capable of receiving only "milk, and not solid food." Filled with a desire to get to the matter, [p. 10] I decided to travel to Liverpool, where a Mormon Church had been established since 1839, so that I might learn English and make myself acquainted with all the Mormon scriptures. Erastus Snow approved and supported my decision; but fate willed otherwise, for while I was waiting for a steamship bound for Liverpool to put in at Copenhagen, a letter arrived for E. Snow from Captain Larsen in Norway, with a request that he send over some elders there. It was a new call from Macedonia: "Come over and help us!" The letter was read aloud before the council of the brethren, and the apostle expressed it as his opinion and desire that I should go to Norway instead of England. Since obedience is a prime duty for a Christian and especially for a Mormon, I declared that I was willing to change my decision. He therefore ordained me as an elder, and soon I was on my journey to Norway in partnership with Elder H. P. Pedersen from Aalborg.

Mormonism made good progress in Norway; many believed and were baptized. In various cities flourishing

---

7. *Doctrine and Covenants,* originally published in 1833 as the *Book of Commandments.* In 1835 it was reprinted with additional contents under the title *Doctrine and Covenants.* The first section in the 1835 edition contained a series of lectures on theology that comprised the "doctrine" element of the *Doctrine and Covenants.* The second part contained the revelations or covenants of the church. Later the lectures were removed as they taught that God was omnipresent and that there were two persons in the Godhead, teachings that conflicted with later Mormon theology. Extensive alterations were also made in many of the revelations. For a detailed study of the changes, see John W. Fitzgerald, "A Study of the Doctrine and Covenants," Master's thesis, BYU, 1940).

churches were established, for example in East Riis Islands. But suddenly opposition arose from an unexpected quarter, that is from the national government. Norwegians have a free choice of religion, to be sure, but not a completely unrestricted choice as the Danes have. That is, the law required that all dissenters (those who differ from the state church) are first to send a petition concerning this to the government in Christiania—which will grant approval to the petition, provided it regards the sect as Christian; but in the opposite case it would reject it. It naturally followed that such a petition was sent in due time by "the Church of Jesus Christ of the Latter Day Saints," but the government of Department of Church Affairs found the matter to be dubious and referred it to the theological faculty.* The theologians found the new religion to be more dubious and speculated for a long time and in vain as to whether it was Christian or not. Finally the very capable and daring official in Smaalehnene, Birch Reichenwald, took the matter in hand and forced a decision. Since some of the missionaries had once met with him and in all simplicity explained their intentions to him, he had them all arrested without further ceremony [p. 11] and confined in the city jail in Frederiksstad. They were four Danes and two Norwegians, among whom was Captain Larsen, who had in his enthusiasm given up his business in order to preach the new gospel.

*i.e., of the University of Christiania. —Trans.

While this was going on in the east country (Østlandet) I was in East Riis Islands in the west country. The report of the arrests however soon reached us, but at the same time I received a courteous request to go up to the city bailiff, who informed me that he had received orders from the authorities in Smaalehnene to have me arrested and taken to Frederiksstad in the steamship "Constitution," which put in at towns by the fjord in its route from Bergen to Christiania.

The city bailiff, whose name I do not now remember, was incidentally a very honorable old man. He was just as surprised at these orders as I was, and he only desired my word that I would give myself up when the "Constitution" put in at the harbor. Finally the steamer arrived and I met it on time, and had as inexpensive and comfortable a tour as possible along the eastern coastland with its variegated cliff scenery, until we arrived at Frederiksstad. Except for the fact that I had to report to the authorities in Moss, there was nothing in my condition otherwise that could remind me that I was under arrest.

In Frederiksstad I was received by the assistant bailiff of the city, I. Fjelstad, who after a short stay in the bailiff's office took me up to my future residence, the city's municipal jail. Amusingly enough, a very delightful surprise awaited me here. That is, I had reckoned on sitting in a dark and lonesome prison, but instead of that the good old assistant bailiff brought me in even to my "brethren in the faith" who had been arrested earlier, to a light and rather comfortable room.

After our case had proceeded at a snail's pace from the southern secretariat to the superior court, which issued its finding in our favor, the city bailiff took it to the Supreme Court. There the matter rested quietly until the autumn of 1852, and our case was lost. The theological faculty had also in the meantime delivered its report, which among other things included the remarkable but appropriate allegation that "Mormonism" [p. 12] was a "political system" which resulted in founding "a kingdom within a kingdom, a state within a state."[c] Although our imprisonment was as mild as possible, yet it appeared to our fellow-prisoner Captain S. Larsen (along with several respected Norwegians who had decided for Mormonism) that Norwegian freedom did not altogether correspond to their own ideas in this direction. As Norwegian citizens with the inborn national pride of every Norwegian, this appeared to them vexatious without any doubt, that they should see themselves along with their friends persecuted and imprisoned on account of their faith. Intensified protests and petitions therefore went forth from the jail in Frederiksstad to the government in Christiania, with an appeal for the justification of the Church of Jesus Christ of the Latter Day Saints. But the goddess of justification seemed to continue turning away from us with her eyes closed and cold expression on her face. She had just as little an ear for our prayers as for our songs, which daily rose in swelling tones from the

---

c. At the same time Mormonism was likewise declared in Hamburg to be "dangerous to the state," and its missionaries were expelled from the city.

second floor of the City Hall. But if that dear goddess had no ear for us imprisoned Mormons, yet she seemed to give much greater attention to the capable bailiff Smaalehnene. And there was now not the slightest doubt that the state official, Birch Reichenwald, and the blind goddess looked more deeply into things than we did, even though it was not so easy to perceive the way. That which also contributed to making the time tolerable for us was the great freedom of movement which Fjeldstad, the old assistant bailiff, granted us. He was a widower and the oldest of his three daughters remaining at home managed the household, and he was the majordomo of the family. Although the old man could not avoid listening to his prisoners' explanation of their faith, yet he was too old and experienced a man of the world to allow himself to be carried away by it. As men who were in the best years of our youth, full of hope and vital religious enthusiasm, we did not appear to the old man at all repellant,—but [p. 13] he could not stomach American Mormonism in any way, and it was also for that reason that he was opposed to his oldest daughter's engagement to the author of this book. But as is apt to happen in such cases, his opposition accomplished nothing. She became my wife, and after the passage of so many years we still often call to mind those days of hope and youthfulness. When the bailiff offered us our freedom finally, upon certain conditions, his offer was accepted, and after seven long months of imprisonment, the last of us forsook the hospitable city jail of Frederiksstad. In November 1853 at the same time that the judgment of the Supreme Court was made known, I forsook Norway and journeyed back to Copenhagen.

During my missionary tour in Norway Mormonism had undergone a substantial change in the capital of Denmark. "The doctrine of polygamy"[8] had been announced as a divine revelation, and although it was known as yet only in a very modified form, nevertheless it had a disturbing and demoralizing effect upon many of the elders as well as upon the Church as a whole.

Willard Snow, who had succeeded his brother, Erastus, as president of the Mission, died. He became demented

---

8. The doctrine of plural marriage is found in section 132 of the *Doctrine and Covenants*.

and died in that state while on a trip from Copenhagen to England. Thereupon John Van Cott became president of the Mission and gave the impression of being a capable and believing man who must have earlier belonged to the "better class" in America, but he still did not understand the Danish language. It was my determination when I left Norway to travel from Copenhagen the ensuing year with a large number of emigrants to Salt Lake City in Utah, but under the unhappy condition of the Church abovementioned, Mr. John Van Cott urgently requested me to stay in Denmark until he himself was relieved of the mission. This gave me some hesitation;—that is to say, I had become engaged and had gone to some expense already at Trinity Church in order to get married according to "the law of the land" in accordance with the wishes of my fiancee's father, the assistant bailiff Fjelstad in Frederiksstad; yet that was taken [p. 14] care of satisfactorily, and I had my wedding on the 9th of December 1853, whereupon I was sent as a traveling elder over the whole Mission. At that time the Mormon congregations in Denmark were organized into six "conferences," each of which was governed by a president. It now became my duty to be on hand at the semiannual sessions of these conferences, in order to see to it that everything was done according to the teachings of the Church and its ordinances, etc. None of the many people who knew me at that time will deny that I carried out my commission according to my best ability and judgment; that is to say, I had embraced the truth of the faith and adhered to it still with all my heart, despite the fact that Mormonism was gradually taking on new forms with new (and until then, completely unheard of) doctrines. Among them the revelation concerning polygamy was a serious stumbling block, even though it was still presented in such a vague and mystic light that it seemed more calculated for blessed spirits than actual people, and of course it did not come into practical use in Denmark; but the worst feature of the matter was that the Mormons had up until that time denied the existence of such a doctrine.[9] This was what one in plain language

---

9. In fact, Joseph Smith also publicly denied the doctrine even though he was privately teaching and practicing it. As mayor of Nauvoo, Illinois, he even had a local newspaper (the *Nauvoo Expositor*) destroyed that accused him of presenting a revelation on polygamy.

calls a deliberate lie, but the Mormon apostles had not read the Bible for nothing. Abraham made Pharaoh believe that Sarah was his sister, and just the same he was called the father of believers. How could a little story like that, adapted to a loving Christian purpose in order not to arouse resentment, be laid to the charge of a Mormon apostle? On the whole they claimed, as it had also become an actual fact, that one could only come to the depths of Mormon doctrine by journeying to "Zion," where "the prophet of the Lord" was, and where His holy temple was to be built. This Zion was not only represented as a place of refuge for the saints, where they would escape the wrath of the Lord that for a long time would be visited upon the nations of earth on account of their sins, but also assurance had been given that there were certain "spiritual gifts" which could be received only there. What these spiritual gifts really consisted of could not be clarified; it was only known that they were reserved with the higher orders of priesthood and were called bestowments or the sealing for "time and eternity." These [p. 15] secret gifts of counsel were called in English "Endowment," and the place where they were imparted was called the "Endowment House." We will come back later to this institution,[10] but the reader nevertheless gets an idea here of how well organized the Mormons' method of procedure really was so that their proselytes, in order to attain the most important and glorious gifts of counsel, first had to travel to Utah and give themselves over wholly and completely to the Mormons' power.

People sometimes speculate about how it is possible that any person of sound mind can convert to Mormonism, and the attempt has been made to counter Mormonism with observations to the effect that its adherents are a crowd of unenlightened and ignorant people. Quite possibly, but what do arguments like that accomplish? Nothing. Did the first Christian church consist of the most educated of their

---

Smith and his brother emphatically denied the charge and testified before the city council that the accusations were untrue. The paper, therefore, was declared a public nuisance and was destroyed (see the Nauvoo *Neighbor,* June 19, 1844.) Eight years later, the Mormon church published the revelation on plural marriage that Smith had received. Thus the newspaper was condemned on the basis of false testimony given by Joseph and Hyrum Smith.

10. See chapter 9.

time, perhaps, or of the most worldly people? Was not Christ's teaching an offense to the Jews who were learned in Scripture, "a foolishness" to the philosophical Greeks? And yet it triumphed over both the Greeks and the Romans. Mormonism is not stupidity or dementia: on the contrary it is an excellently elaborated system for bringing people under a perfectly despotic priestly power. But only with extreme caution and only gradually is this imparted to proselytes. Not until after a sojourn in Utah does the matter become clear to him, and thus it is that one can draw himself back from it only with great difficulty. It is significant that Mormonism first appeared in America. Enlightenment and national freedom for the most part should go hand in hand, [but]* they often stand in striking contrast with each other—as is well known—and consequently the mass of the American people are almost always inclined to go in for any kind of humbug at all with incredible heedlessness and are willing to work in the service of the humbug with the "Yankees'" own perseverance and energy. In a country where weeds or vices can rear their heads and call themselves "Freedom and Equality," that is where Mormonism may first be rightly understood and perceived. That which in other lands must be regarded as something unheard of and incredible appears here as something perfectly natural, as something which belongs to the order of the day.

*This word added for clarity. —Trans.

2 The Journey to Utah

[p. 16] In an attractive and almost poetic way the yearning desire to "go home to Zion" appeared in Mormonism. Many of the Psalms express this in moving terms, and on every occasion the apostles emphasized the new Zion with its rich promises. It was therefore only natural that the saints looked forward with great impatience to the day when they could begin their journey to Utah, even though the departure from their native land must at times have weighed heavily upon their hearts.

On the twenty-third of April 1856, one hundred sixty-two Mormons departed from Copenhagen on the steamship Rhoda. The author of this little book was appointed as the leader of this society of emigrants over the North Sea. On the thirtieth of April we arrived at Liverpool in good condition; there we joined up with six hundred eight English and Scottish Mormons who also stood ready to "go home to Zion." Then finally on the fourth of May our journey over the Atlantic Ocean with the ship Thronton had its beginning. It is not my intention here to give a description of something nowadays so well known as a voyage by sea in an emigrant ship. We Mormons suffered no greater inconveniences on board than other emigrants do under the same circumstances—perhaps even fewer, for a well-conceived organization, in which the Latter Day Saints have always excelled, was not lacking among us even on shipboard. Franklin D. Richards in Liverpool, one of the twelve apostles of the new Zion, and President of the European Mission, had named a president and three advisors to maintain oversight of the saints during the journey.

[p. 17] An elder named G. J. Willie[1] was appointed as president. Milton Atwood, Moses Clough, and I were the advisers. Besides that, nothing noteworthy occurred during our long and rather stormy crossing except that one might perhaps include six deaths, three births, and—two marriages as well.

On the fourteenth of June we landed in New York, where the apostle John Taylor[2] received us, and under his leadership our journey from that point on was continued to Iowa City, which is located about thirteen hundred English miles east of Salt Lake City and had a population of about three thousand. It had some importance as an exit point for a significant emigration. That is to say, the railroad lines stopped at that point; if one wished to go farther west, the journey had to be continued by other means. The usual means of conveyance consisted naturally of wagons, which were drawn by horses, mules, or oxen; but this year the prophet Brigham Young had just made a discovery along this line. That is to say, considerable expense was involved in conveying the usually indigent emigrants over the prairies in the customary fashion, and so he hit upon the idea that the emigrants themselves should pull their own wagons. Upon our arrival in Iowa City a team of Mormons was found busily engaged in constructing a kind of two-wheeled vehicle (handcart) that weighed about sixty pounds, and each of these wagons was allotted to five persons with seventeen pounds of baggage apiece, which consisted of the most necessary articles of clothing and cooking vessels. Emigrants of larger means naturally preferred to travel in the customary way, and that is what I did as well. But F. D. Richards had requested me to escort the indigent Danes with their train of handcarts, since I was the only one of them who had any competence in English.

---

1. James G. Willie.
2. John Taylor. He later succeeded Brigham Young as President of the Mormon church.

After I had arranged for my wife to go with a conventional train of vehicles with which a portion of the Danish emigrants had joined, I also fulfilled that request of his, even though it was obvious that that journey would prove extremely difficult.

The handcart train, which consisted of about five hundred persons, broke camp by Iowa City on the sixteenth [p. 18] of July 1856, with twenty-three tents, ninety-four handcarts, and five large provision wagons. G. D. Willie took over the leadership again and divided us up into five sections. For each section there was one large wagon drawn by three yoke of oxen that carried the provisions and the tents. The provisions were calculated according to a daily ration for each man at one pound of wheat flour, two-and-a-half ounces of meat, two ounces of sugar, two ounces of dried apples, one quarter ounce of coffee, along with a little tea, soda, and soap.

The fifth division consisted of ninety-three Scandinavians, for which I was appointed leader; but the honor connected with this post was slight, and the advantages even less than that. That is, it led to my having to drive the wagon myself with the three yoke of oxen, [for]* none of *This word the others seemed able to drive it, and that is also a diffi-   added for cult piece of work besides, when one has no reins to guide   clarity. the animals with, but only a long whip and certain stereo-   —Trans. typed expressions in ox-language. By the middle of August we reached Florence, a little town situated on the west bank of the Missouri River, which was at that time a boundary between the territory of the "red men" and that of the "palefaces." Here I met up with Elder Van Cott along with several prominent missionaries who were on their journey home to Salt Lake City from their various missions in Europe and Asia.

We also received there a number of beef cattle, which were to provide us with meat for the rest of the journey, to be slaughtered as we had need of them.

Since we were still a thousand miles away, many who were acquainted with the climatic conditions of the region were of the opinion that we ought to winter in Florence. But the oldest son of the prophet H. E. Kimball[3] then rode into camp and delivered a speech in which he sternly

---

3. Heber C. Kimball, counselor to Brigham Young.

rebuked those of little faith, and he promised that he would "stuff into his mouth all the snow they would ever get to see on their journey to the valleys!" With this of course every doubt had to vanish altogether. Captain Willie also stated that he would continue the trip until he received orders from Brigham Young to desist.

The journey was resumed. On August twenty-ninth we reached Fort Kearney and visited the chief of the Omaha Indians, who was staying in the camp with his tribe. The savages were smoking, and very obligingly handed us the peace-pipe [p. 19] by way of compensation for a few presents (an entire portion of dried buffalo meat) their chief accepted. We were told here that a small party that belonged to Secretary Babbit[a] had been murdered by a band of "Cheyenne Indians." We also reached the place on the following day and found the burned-out wagons, with the corpses of two men and a child. On the thirty-first we were overtaken by Secretary Babbit himself, who was returning home from a visit to Washington. He now had only his coachman and a lady with a little child along with him. He said that with the exception of these "Cheyennes" he was personally acquainted with every Indian tribe between the Missouri River and Utah.

He had traveled this way several times, on one occasion all alone—and he now believed himself to be perfectly certain of getting through successfully despite the misfortune that had overtaken the men who were carrying his baggage. After a short stay with us he set off again at a gallop relying on his hardy, light-footed mules and his own experience.

From there we went on to Nebraska's enormous prairieland, which stretches from the Missouri River to the Rocky Mountains—about 500 miles. The way proceeds almost the whole time alongside the Platte River, which runs from west to east in a valley which is ten to fifteen miles in some places. The land seemed fertile, that is, it has a rich growth of grass, but because of the annual prairie fire which sweeps across the plain neither trees nor bushes are to be found there, except here or there,

---

a. President Fillmore had already recognized Utah in 1851 as a territory in the Union and had named Brigham Young as governor there, along with Babbit as Secretary. Babbit, incidentally, was an apostate from Mormonism.

where a little river with its curving banks has managed to halt the all-destroying rage of the fire king. Our journey went quite well until the third of September, but on that day an unhappy event took place there which later on caused us much suffering and the death of many men. It was already evening when we made camp, and the darkness was intensified still more by a fearful storm which raged on through the whole night. Shortly before the storm broke loose, many [p. 20] of us heard a strange noise which seemed like the sound of wagons driving swiftly by; but since nothing like that showed itself, we assumed that it originated from a passing herd of buffalo, and we went to sleep. The next morning it appeared that in the meantime twenty-two oxen, the majority of our draught animals, had disappeared, and their very tracks had been obliterated by the rain. It often happens in these extensive plains, where the animals seem to recall something of their original wildness, that oxen, mules, and horses when frightened suddenly dash off as if possessed. If one can follow after them immediately on a good horse until they come to a halt through exhaustion, then he may sometimes get them back; but it is impossible to halt them before that. Such a flight of animals is called a "stampede." We never saw the oxen again, even though we waited three days to look for them. There were now only twelve oxen left, except for the slaughter cattle previously mentioned, which consisted of cows and calves. We were now forced to try, even though it did little good, to employ these as draught animals. The end result was that some of the provisions had to be loaded on the handcarts and in that fashion we resumed our journey; but progress was slow, very slow indeed.

On the eighteenth of September early in the morning, before my night watch was over, I saw a horseman approach our camp. At first I took him for an Indian, but with a closer look he showed himself to be clothed in a military uniform, and so taken as a whole, he seemed to be an American soldier. He related that he had traveled from Fort Laramie in company with two families who had left Utah[b] in order to return to the States. While he had gone

b. The names of the two families were Margetts and Coudy. They were "apostates" on their way to England, and it is suspected that "Bill Hickman" with two other Mormons was sent out to execute the murder. Consult *Mormonism* by John Hyde.

off in the morning of the previous day in order to shoot a buffalo, the Indians had murdered all the rest. Upon his return he found the wagons in flames [p. 21] and the corpses of his companions, five adults and a baby. After that he continued his journey full of horror and went about seventy miles across the prairie without stopping until he came to us. Secretary Babbit and his three henchmen were likewise murdered by "Cheyenne Indians." On Sunday the eighteenth of October the first snow fell, but on that same day we met three wagons laden with provisions that had been sent out from Salt Lake City. Our pitiful plight had become known there, since several Mormon dignitaries had driven past us in carriages on the way and had furnished the information about this to Brigham Young. Joseph A. Young (Brigham's oldest son), whose acquaintance I had already made in Denmark, was the leader of this train. The provisions were, however, not intended for us but for two trains of emigrants who were still farther behind. We were comforted by the information that on the following day we would meet fourteen wagons with provisions which were intended for us. This was a joyful message, and Young was rewarded with repeated cheers when he parted from us. That evening we set up camp by a small river called "Sweetwater," and we confidently distributed the scraps of food we still had left, consisting of a meager portion of store-bread that we had bought in Laramie. Our rations had already been reduced a good while before, until they shrank to six ounces of meal per day; the coffee and tea had long since been used up. We thought we had now survived the worst, but now cold and nakedness were added to hunger and overstrain! As we remained encamped about evening beside the afore-mentioned small stream, the warmth of the sun had melted the snow away, and we went to sleep with good hopes concerning the future. But the next morning we woke up with a different feeling. During the night the snow had fallen a foot deep, and the area around Sweetwater, which under no circumstances looks very inviting, now appeared doubly desolate and comfortless. Our last provisions had been distributed and as for the animals, where were they to find fodder?

Three days slipped by but no wagons came, and so we sent out two men to see whether they had possibly driven in the wrong direction and passed us by. Finally [p. 22] the relief train arrived on the evening of the twenty-first of October, under the leadership of the aforementioned snow prophet, George Kimball. His courage was hardly as great now as it had been in Florence, but the necessary cocksureness in the character of the son of the Mormon prophet was by no means lacking in him. Captain Willie immediately took his leave, and Kimball himself assumed leadership over the emigrant train. The provisions and articles of clothing were distributed, but they were unfortunately far from adequate in the grim winter that had now begun.

Captain Kimball had now decided to make forced marches. He had the whole plan all figured out in his mind how this was going to be done, and he was a man for carrying it out. On the twenty-third of October we broke camp from Sweetwater in the following order. First, the children, the old people, and the sick who could still move about marched off under the leadership of a certain renowned Copenhager, Mursvend Christensen.[c] So these two-wheeled infernal machines invented by Brigham Young came along, drawn by exhausted men and women. The vehicles brought up the rear for this miserable procession. This order of travel did not, however, last very long, because many began to fall behind quite soon with their handcarts, which were incapable of keeping up in the order which Kimball had initiated. There was a Dane named Niels Andersen, who had shown himself during almost the entire trip to be one of the strongest and bravest in the entire train. He had often loaded his fourteen-year old daughter on his cart when she was tired, and yet he still drove ahead just as happily with her. But more recently he had been attacked by dysentery, which had begun to spread to an alarming extent. By this day it had befallen Christensen's group, and his wife had to pull their cart by herself. Naturally she [p. 23] had fallen behind, and I therefore gave her a helping hand until we reached our camp location. It went pretty well that way, but we could not overtake the caravan. It was just about noon however,

---

c. He came from the western states on a mission from Utah and had joined us in Florence. Later he was accused of murdering a deaf and dumb servant while he was appointed as postmaster in Salt Lake City. He even confessed the murder, but he was released. The reason for the murder could never be explained by the judges.

when we came up to her husband, who was tottering along the road and seemed as helpless as a child. He broke out with heartrending lamentation when he saw us. His wife comforted him as well as she could and gave him some food, which he ate ravenously. We stopped in order to wait for some wagons that were still farther behind, to have them pick him up as they drove by. Finally Savage came, the captain of the wagons, with a ox-drawn wagon; but he refused to take Niels Andersen up because the wagon, as he said, was already overloaded. After a serious discussion with me, and after he had become convinced by personal examination of him that the man could walk no farther, he brought himself after all to pick him up. This day of forced marching also came to an end, but not until two hours after it had become dark, did we arrive, in company with one of the Utah wagons with which we had caught up. We came to the campsite where the earlier arrivals had already kindled a fire and set up their tents. By midnight the last Utah wagon came in; but since several of the handcarts were still missing, some of the wagons were sent off to help them, and it was 4:30 A.M. when the last of them returned.

The next morning, which was therefore October twenty-fourth, fourteen emigrants were found frozen dead in our camp, among whom was Niels Andersen. Two more died later on in the day.[4] They were all buried in a large rectangular grave, which because of the cold had to be dug out in the ground by oxen. This was the first fruit of the forced march of George Kimball, the snow prophet. The resentment toward him was quite general; I myself was simple-minded enough to threaten him that I would present a complaint against him to Brigham Young! Oh, you trusting simpleton! The prophet laughed right in my face. It was no longer necessary for him to wear the mask of his counterfeit holiness. Through the Mormon sheep's fleece the wolf's claws were beginning to show. Although the trip proceeded in a more sensible manner, yet from then on almost every one of our natural campsites was marked [p. 24] by a fresh grave.[5] God knows how many of us there

---

4. These deaths were noted in the *Comprehensive History of the Church,* 3:93.

5. Mormon Historian O. H. Roberts numbers the total deaths at 77 (see *Comprehensive History of the Church,* 3:94).

were who would have escaped with our lives if from Salt Lake City, where our sorrowful condition was well known, Brigham Young had sent the one relief train after the other in order to bring us in. When we reached Fort Bridges (one hundred twenty miles from Salt Lake City) we didn't have to use those two-wheeled man-tormentors anymore, and anyone who felt the need could get a ride. On the eighth of December after passing over the Big Mountain we looked down for the first time on the valleys where the Lord's people had taken up residence, and where the promises which awaited them were to be fulfilled. Many forgot the tribulations they had endured upon glimpsing this sudden vista, and on the following day, which was a Sunday, we all broke formation, and as we exchanged expressions of eager anticipation we drove down speedily through the twelve miles of the long, snow-free Emigration Canyon to the great Salt Sea Valley, where we caught sight of Salt Lake City, seven miles distant, the capital city of Mormonism and Brigham Young. From that distance the city with its light gray adobe houses looked like a huge encampment, and the Salt Lake Valley, which had a breadth of about thirty miles from east to west, resembled a basin or dried up lake, with its huge mountain masses ranging upward on all sides.

Although the vegetation was now dead, and the eye of the observer met only a desolate treeless valley, surrounded by bare, reddish mountains, yet the impression made by the whole scene was still very pleasing. The climate was still mild and pleasant down there, and the enormous cliffs and mountain masses, which towered skyward on every side, gave way to an impressive, almost romantic, appearance.

In the afternoon our wagon train reached the city. As we came to a halt just in front of the palace of Brigham Young, the bishops and many of the ministers of the nearby Tabernacle came up. The prophet did not honor us with a personal visit; presumably he was ashamed to look upon our miserable and wretched condition, the result of his own shortsighted and ill-conceived plan, but he had bidden his bishops to hold themselves in readiness for our arrival, in order to take care of billeting us in their various districts in the city. [p. 25] I myself was soon surrounded with several old acquaintances from Denmark who had been living for some time in Utah. They took me to their own homes with great friendliness—after my traveling companions (most of whom I saw for the last time) had been provided with lodging.

The last emigrant train of this year, namely Martin's Handcart Company, and the Independent Wagon Company to which my wife belonged, arrived at Salt Lake City on the seventeenth of December in a condition (if possible) even worse than our own. The wagon company had lost nearly all its draught animals and consequently had to leave their goods behind and their wagons as well along the way. They left some of them behind in Laramie, but the greater part of them were in Fort Bridge or by the Devil's Gate. It was one of the severest winters ever known. The snow lay a foot deep in the valleys and about two or three feet on the mountains. I had been very anxious about my wife and little son and tried in every way to get myself sent out with a departing relief train to meet them, but in vain. I only succeeded in sending a buffalo hide and a little coffee and sugar with the wagons, which were supposed to bring them to them. The buffalo hide she received, but nothing else. On the seventeenth of December I went personally to meet the wagon company and reached them at the base of Little Mountains. Who could describe my joy at finding both of my dear ones in the best of health? Forgotten were the hardships of the journey and the long separation, and joyfully we drove in to Zion.

3 Salt Lake City

[p. 26] Salt Lake City is one of many valleys or "basins" which have been built up by the Mormons in Utah Territory. The Great Salt Lake lies in this valley northwest of the city which bears its name.[a] As its name indicates, its water is saline and contains a proportion of twenty to twenty-two percent of salt depending upon the seasons, whether wet or dry. During fall and winter, when the water levels are at their lowest, one can walk along the flat beach and find a thick layer of crystalline salt. The lake receives its supply of water from the numerous rivers descending from the surrounding mountain ranges. There is no visible outlet, and so it is assumed to be a survival of a huge inland sea which in times long past completely filled the Great Basin, which in connection with larger and smaller valleys extends about five hundred miles from north to south, three hundred miles from east to west, and lies about four thousand feet above sea level. South of the Salt Lake Valley and separated from it by only two projecting ranges of mountains which allow for an open pass there lies the attractive

---

a. Here, as in all other places in this book, distances are given in English miles.

Utah Valley with its lovely fresh-water lake of the same name. The famous Jordan River has its origin at Utah Lake; its outlet on the other hand finds its way to the Great Salt Lake.

The Salt Sea Valley and the Utah Valley are the largest in the Territory and in 1870 had a combined population of 31,791 inhabitants, or about a fourth of all the population of Utah. Salt Lake City is beautifully situated on the west side of the valley along the edge of the mountains. At the time of my arrival there it had about fifteen thousand inhabitants. The majority [p. 27] consisted of immigrants from the Scandinavian countries and Great Britain. Only about a third of the city and a quarter of the Territory's population are native-born Americans, but nevertheless they are the ones who have authority everywhere and are almost exclusively in control of the ecclesiastical and civil offices. Even among the "Saints" the "know-nothing principle" operates to validate itself: "America is to be governed by Americans."

Salt Lake City is laid out with 110-foot wide streets running at right angles north and south, and in this way it forms blocks which are ten acres in size. These again are subdivided into lots large enough to afford room enough for a house and garden. Along the sidewalks of the streets there are pretty deciduous trees which are watered by the water runoff emerging from the irrigated fruit orchards of the city. If the city had all been built according to the original plan, it would have come to resemble a grandiose park installation with broad avenues and a multitude of bungalows; and that is the way it really looks, by the way, except for areas where the population belongs to the working class, or where business life has crowded out the rural appearance. In those days the houses were constructed from a kind of unbaked brick, the so-called adobe; only a few of them were coated over with brown or white cement. Brigham Young's residence took up an entire block, which was surrounded by granite walls eight feet high. His most important palace was called the Beehive House, after a colossal beehive which was installed on the roof. The beehive, incidentally, was the emblem of the Mormons.[1] In this building the prophet had his headquarters,

---

1. The beehive idea was adopted from the *Book of Mormon*, Ether 2:3.

both in his capacity as temporal head of the Territory and as its spiritual head. Here also lived the prophet's first wife and their children.

A little to the north of the Beehive House lies the Lion House, which has a stone lion over its entrance. The "Lion" is Brigham's emblem; that is, he has taken the title "the Lion of the Lord" in the symbolic writings of Mormonism. The Lion House is a kind of harem, a residence for seventeen or eighteen of Brigham's secondary wives and their respective children. Both of these houses are surrounded by delightful fruit orchards and are said to have cost $95,000 all together. In the same block [p. 28] is located the Tithe House of the Church along with its connected stores and warehouses.

North of the prophet's block lies the so-called Temple Block, which is likewise surrounded by a wall ten feet high with four gates, with the embellishment of lovely deciduous trees. Inside the wall is located the Tabernacle, which was the principal church of the city and of the denomination. Here the Saints assembled two times each Sunday in order to hear "Brother Brigham" and other prominent Mormons preach.[2] The building accommodates about three thousand people, and it is built inside in the form of a large amphitheater, with rows of chairs rising above one another in a terraced fashion. In the vicinity of the Tabernacle there is a low, unimpressive house, but one which nevertheless has its importance, for it is the aforementioned Endowment House.[3] Since that time a large new Tabernacle has been erected which from the standpoint of its architecture is certainly unique. That is, the most outstanding feature about the building is a huge round roof, which on the whole bears a resemblance to a ship's hull of shallow construction which with the cassock in the air rests upon a multitude of pillars. In addition to the capacious, terraced floor there is a gallery. At the one end of the nave is a kind of ground floor installed for the priests. This is divided into three rooms, each of which has its speaker's or preacher's chair, which is in the form of a semicircle standing out from the rows of other chairs. The

---

2. Many of these sermons can be read today in the *Journal of Discourses,* 26 vols. (Liverpool: Asa Calkin, 1854-86). Photo reprint available from Deseret Bookstore, Salt Lake City, Utah.

3. See page 14 (of the Danish work) and chapter 9.

first preacher's chair is for Brigham Young and the high dignitaries of the Church, the second and third chair for the lesser luminaries. Behind the preacher's platform rises an enormous, especially impressive organ, which is said to have cost $100,000. The entire building accommodates about twelve thousand people.

In the Temple Block are found also the beginnings of the much discussed "Temple." The ground wall—and that is about all one can see now—is very massive and lies about sixteen feet deep. To be sure, the prophet has collected enormous sums among the saints for the "Temple construction," but yet he seems to be in no hurry to see it built. Perhaps he remembers the fate of the [p. 29] great Mormon temple in Nauvoo and he has come to the sensible conclusion that it is safer and more rewarding to put the money into a nice theater, which not only has a better prospect of surviving a possibly impending emigration elsewhere, but also contributes two temporal benefits that Brigham Young knows how to appreciate very much: *money* and *enjoyments*.

Besides the aforementioned religious buildings there is also within the Temple block a kind of mechanical workshop, or, as it is called, a Public Works, where the Church has various items of iron and wood manufactured. Here there are many European craftsmen employed, who of course receive their wages from the Church's Tithe House.

East of Brigham Young's residence and in the vicinity of the Temple grounds lies the "Little City" of the prophet Heber C. Kimball. This is formed of a group of houses, some large and some small, which are used by his "little family" consisting of seventeen or eighteen wives with a corresponding number of children! Kimball was Brigham's "first adviser" and therefore the second greatest man in the Church. His residences, although numerous and large in area, are lacking in all that elegant style and decoration which mark those of Brigham Young and the dwellings of other less distinguished persons. Kimball was also a great man with a great faith, [but]* he preferred strength to beauty. For his discourses, which I often had the honor of listening to, he had the following standard and all-embracing texts: "Brigham Young's authority," "the divine authority of the priesthood," "Brigham Young, as the head of the Church and the Lord's anointed," etc. etc.,

*This word added for clarity. —Trans.

with the necessary consequence that people could only be prospered and be saved by means of the power and the spiritual life that issued from that mighty fountain of power![4]

But it was the city that we were supposed to give a little sketch of. Besides the buildings already mentioned the city had at that time only a few other points of interest, yet it offered a living example of the industry and exertion of this people, and it furnished an unmistakable evidence of the power of man and civilization over nature. For out of the barren wilderness were brought forth flourishing gardens and fertile [p. 30] fields. The soil in that city as everywhere in the valleys is very fruitful after it has simply been irrigated with water; thus the whole city is watered by a small stream which emerges from Brigham's Canyon and from which by the aid of trenches is led across the entire city. Since it rains only seldom in these regions, one finds towns and settlements only in such locations as those where greater or smaller streams run down through the deep and snowy mountain passes, or where one can with the help of trenches dam up the water and lead it across the flat and sloping plains in the valleys. In the lower portions of the valley a heavy overgrowth of grass is found because of the natural moisture of the soil. But even there large stretches are found which are completely sterile because of the mineral soda or "alkali" which covers the ground, and it is a destructive poison for both plants and animals. In Utah Valley no forest trees are found, nor even upon the nearby mountain slopes, but high up on the nearest inaccessible mountain summits spruce trees grow and flourish. This in short is the way the land looks which is the home of the Mormons in America.

---

4. In a discourse delivered on July 29, 1856, Kimball stated, "I have not come to do my will, but to do the will of him that sent me, even that of brother Brigham." (*Journal of Discourses*, 4:2). For other statements by Heber Kimball concerning Brigham Young's authority, see *Journal of Discourses*, 1:206; 4:1-3, 66, 171; 5:334.

4 The Mormons in Utah

In September 1849 Utah was admitted as a territory in the Union, and Brigham Young was appointed by President Fillmore of the United States as governor of the territory and superintendent for the local Indian tribes. The Mormons thereby secured the right of sending a representative to Congress and electing their own legislative assembly and at the same time of installing certain subordinate officials, all of whom would be salaried by the United States government The Governor, the Secretary, and the top judges, on the other hand were appointed in Washington. In the meantime, since the territorial form of government [p. 31] is regarded as only a period of minority for a state, the Mormons have tried ever since 1849 to become admitted into the Union as a "free, independent state" by the name of "Deseret." This continual petitioning, incidentally, was not based upon any special loyalty or love of theirs toward the Union, but only upon their desire to govern themselves and carry on their own unlawful deeds without having to fear foreign interference. A republic with the motto Freedom and Equality and six or seven million slaves could otherwise be taken as queer enough, but the Mormon state "Deseret" with a "prophet" as governor would be an even worse satire—one of the greatest humbugs America could ever expect to produce.

From an ecclesiastical or religious perspective—and that is really the essence of Mormonism—Utah is ruled by a completely despotic hierarchy. Brigham Young is the supreme head of the Church with the title of prophet, seer, etc. His power is unlimited, for he is the representative of the Almighty on earth.[1] In association with two so-called advisers he forms the highest presidency of the Church. Next in rank follow "the Twelve Apostles" with their president at the head. The Apostles are a kind of envoys who stand at the prophet's command, as his representatives in foreign lands or outlying portions of his own domain. Next come an innumerable herd of "high priests," "bishops," "seventies," and "elders" with their organizations and presidents. They make up the higher or Melchizedek priesthoods. The lesser or "Aaronic priesthoods" consist of "priests," "teachers," "deacons" and include virtually all the rest of the male population of the Mormon Church.

Although there are few people in the Mormon Society who are not "ordained" to one of the offices above named, yet the governing and executive power in the Mormon hierarchy is in the hands of very few.

Thus Salt Lake City is divided up into twenty or more districts, and for each of these a "bishop" is appointed, who with his two advisers governs with the same [p. 32] authority in his district as Brigham does over the entire Church. Every city, every settlement in Utah is administered by bishops, whose duty it is not only to preach "the everlasting Gospel" but in particular to collect the church tithes and maintain control over the church's spiritual and temporal means and properties in their respective bishoprics.

The bishops stand immediately under Brigham Young's leadership and are chosen with regard to their unconditional reliability and obedience to him. They receive their instructions from the prophet and send in their reports to him, and like him they combine in themselves an authority both political and ecclesiastical.

This is the political setup of the Mormons, but like all

---

1. Speaking of Brigham Young, Heber Kimball stated "his instructions are the word of God to us" (*Journal of Discourses*, 4:2).

other despots the prophet has his secret police, or his private murder gangs completely compliant to his will, who in line with the rest of their sanctity are called "Danites" or "destroying angels"—Porter Rootwell* and Bill Hickman have become notorious in the history of the Mormon community as the commanders of these gangs.[2] The sinister feature about this system is that it is permeated by an inescapable spy system, which like a poisonous lizard slithers about and nourishes itself in every family. For the harm that the Society suffers from in its health extends itself quite naturally into the family circles as well—the Yankees, who have an unusual readiness to judge things on the basis of externals according to their immediate material interests, sometimes have busied themselves with idolizing Brigham Young* because of the great material advances which Utah has made under his leadership. His administrative ability has been emphasized as something unique, which possibly outweighs the civil and spiritual slavery into which he debased his people. But thousands of other men could have done the same and accomplished the same results if they had been in Brigham Young's place and possessed his avid desire and impudent unscrupulousness. Brigham reaped the glory, but the poor, simple people who in their poverty and want have not only transformed a desert mountain country into a fertile land, but also [p. 33] a poor ignorant Yankee into a millionaire, are hardly even thought of.

*A spelling error by the author. The man's name was Porter Rockwell. —Ed.

*The original text reads "B. Y." —Ed.

We already know in part how Mormonism appeared in Denmark, and now we should briefly turn to an account of how it first made its appearance in its own home. The "Tabernacle" naturally deserves the newcomer's first visit. We came to it and found there, besides a large gathering of "saints," their two prophets also, Brigham Young and Heber C. Kimball. After prayer had been offered and the songs had been sung to the accompaniment of a large orchestra, Orson Hyde, the president of the apostles, stepped forward to discuss the religious questions of the day. He began with the observation (which was rather surprising to us) that "the people in Utah have varying concepts of God," and that "they seem to be uncertain who

---

2. For documentation of the activities of these "murder gangs," see *Mormonism: Shadow or Reality?* pp. 428-50.

their God is," etc. Following that he referred to various passages in Scripture where the designations "God" and "gods" are attributed to Moses and others. His sermon took up the whole time presenting deity as something visible and near at hand, but even though Brother Hyde was an experienced and able speaker who understood very well how to handle his theme, yet he concluded it just about at the same standpoint at which he had begun it, and then he left it to someone else to draw conclusions. Yet we were not doomed to long-continued uncertainty about this important matter, for soon after Orson Hyde an elder named Wheelock stepped forward, and shouted out with all of the exultation of a wretched sycophant, "Brigham Young is my God;—he is good enough for me, and I want no other!"[3]

That was certainly a novel instruction for us newcomers. To be sure, we had heard some talk about Brigham Young's having received a revelation (which is said to be the only one he ever allowed to be announced) which went as follows: "Adam is our father and our God—the only God we have anything to do with!"[4]—but Wheelock's pronouncement was nevertheless too insane. The Prophet, who heard him, certainly would want to make some remonstrance and tell him something different. Brigham Young got to speak that same day, sure enough. After a few unimportant remarks [p. 34] he finally came around to the same theme that Hyde and Wheelock had waded through, as he at first made fun of and ridiculed the orthodox church for believing in a "triune God," and after that he concluded with the following result: "How much more sensible wouldn't it be," he said, "for a people to believe in a righteous man, on whom they have reliance and can seek advice every day!" Yes indeed! We could not clearly sense "the immediate source of divine revelation" by the way in which the new dogmas kept pouring out.

---

3. In a similar statement Heber Kimball declared, "Some have said that I was very presumptuous to say this Brother Brigham was my God and Saviour . . ." (Journal of Wilford Woodruff, April 10, 1852), microfilm available at BYU Library, special collections.
4. In a discourse delivered on April 9, 1852, Young stated that "Adam is our father and God and the only God with whom we have to do" (see Journal of Discourses, 1:50). Young taught this doctrine for over twenty-five years, although the present-day Mormon church denies the teaching. For a study of this strange doctrine see Chris Vlachos, Adam Is God? (Salt Lake City: Utah Lighthouse Ministry).

Brigham customarily has but little to do with abstract religious questions. He has a taste, on the other hand, for practical living, and while he teaches the brethren how to plant cabbage and potatoes, he tells the sisters how they should go about the milking of the cows, the baking of bread and the churning of butter, and so on. Brigham is, incidentally, very clever at conducting his despotism so calculatingly that the people have no idea that he is the one who is their unremitting tax-gatherer. It is not Brigham's hand that crushes the grapes to press out its juice, but in any case one is sure to find the wine in Brigham's cellar.

Upon our later attendance at the Tabernacle we were surprised in a pleasant way by Apostle Lorenzo Snow, who gave a speech which seemed expressly called for by the present and all too obvious circumstances, occasioned by the most recent unhappy handcart immigration. That is to say, he counseled the "saints" and "brothers in Zion" not to "turn their back and look the other way" when they met one of the new arrivals and now helpless immigrants from Europe, for after all, the missionaries in their own time had received hospitality abroad from these poor people, and so now it was befitting, all things considered, for them to show a more active sympathy and involvement such as beseemed a holy people, and so on. For us this speech was a little ray of light in the dark Mormon sky, but it was extinguished like a falling star; for as soon as the apostle had finished, another "authority" whose name I no longer remember, stepped forward and explained in a very commanding tone [p. 35] that there was not to be found anything such as sympathy in Mormonism! There was only "duty and obedience"! That man was, incidentally, quite correct.

Later on, as we often attended the Tabernacle, we came to see that although it was always well filled with people who called themselves saints, yet it was from the spiritual standpoint an empty desert in which the spirit and teaching of Christ have no dwelling place. We perceived also that Mormon doctrine was an unhappy conglomeration that swings like a spiritual chaos helplessly between two opposing foci, namely between the Christian faith and Bible (which is here called "the ancient traditions"), and the revelations of the modern prophet. The question that Mormonism cannot dispose of is whether the American boy with the golden plates is to be preferred to the history of Jesus, the child of Bethlehem.

In each of the districts of the city there is also a meeting-house, in which everyone has a right to step forward and give expression to his inner feelings; otherwise it is conducted by the bishop of the district. Bishop Wooley's meetinghouse was the one most respected in the city, because Brigham and many of the respected Mormon families belong to it, and there we paid our first visit to the meetinghouses. Something we got out of the visit was a proof for the claim that Mormonism possesses all of the spiritual gifts like the first Christian church, for there was a lady who stepped up from the audience and began to speak in a strange "tongue." She showed no sign of an unusual spiritual emotion and appeared to be quite calm, but it was impossible to understand a word of what she said. When she fell silent, the bishop stepped up and asked whether there was anyone to interpret the tongue? No, there was no one who had received "the gift of interpretation," and so the bishop said that although he would rather have understood the "tongue" that the sister concerned had spoken in, yet he understood enough of it to know that "she had praised God in a foreign tongue!" Yet it is in a strange way that God distributes His gifts among these people, for a gift of speaking in tongues that no one understands should be [p. 36] regarded as a curiosity that our Lord would hardly concern Himself with. On the same evening an old, white-haired brother came forward as well who was full of the Spirit and related great visions and revelations which the Lord had shown him. He had seen "Zion besieged by the armies of the heathen," and he saw how their weapons and cannonballs fell harmlessly to earth. Then finally he had seen "one of Israel's warriors chase a thousand heathen in flight as in ancient times."

The third district in the city was made up of the so-called Danish District. The bishop there was a poor old American named Hill, who was married to two hefty young English women who were natural sisters. His first adviser was an old acquaintance, Jensen—or Pottemager Jensen, as he was called—from Horsholm in Denmark. Jensen was an honest man and highly regarded by the Danish population in Salt Lake City. His nature was steady and thoughtful, and his house stood in a pleasant open area where Danish heartiness and hospitality were still kept up, despite the harsh intolerance which invariably derives from Mormonism. Jensen made his living from ceramics and was a good businessman.

Another acquaintance, Jernstøber ["Blacksmith"]* Jensen from Aalborg, who at that time lived in the northern part of the valley in a town named "Vorelder," had just come to town and was supposed to give a lecture about polygamy. He knew about the subject in a practical way, at least, for he had no less than four wives to begin with. It was a matter of course that the Bible had to serve as a model with Abraham, Isaac, and Jacob, but incidentally Jensen, like the Mormons in general, preferred to seek his arguments from nature, and compared, for example, a man who had only one wife with a "rooster who had only one hen" . . . "Or!" he asked triumphantly, "what would you think of a man who plants and sows his field today, and then on the next day begins to plough and harrow it again?" The evidence was decisive; Jensen and plural marriage could not be argued against. Anyone who did not believe in the both and live accordingly was [p. 37] rated quite a bit lower in merit than those who walk on all fours.

*This word added for clarity by translator. The word "Jernstøber" is apparently a nickname.—Ed.

During another visit with our Danish friends in the Third District we received a striking proof of how little regard the Bible enjoys among the "saints." A young Danish brother gave a lecture which went along in a good biblical spirit according to the old custom. But the poor fellow was scarcely through with his sermon than he was admonished in the sharpest scolding way that if he wanted to preach, he would have to come "with clean flour in his pouch, not with old leaven."

In private conversations with acquaintances who had lived for several years in Utah and had consequently gone through the secret levels of Mormonism or the so-called endowment, I also found out that their concepts about the Bible had undergone a complete revolution. Christ was only esteemed like Moses, Joseph Smith, or Brigham.— The biblical accounts of the Lord's punitive judgments upon Korah, Judas, Ananias, and Sapphira, and so on, they explain in such a way that the Almighty had employed for that purpose a band of murderers or an "order"—since it sounds a bit nicer—which existed both in the Mosaic period and in the Christian church like the "destroying angels" or "Danites" among the Mormons.

In agreement with this the Mormons believe and teach that there are certain sins in Zion which can be atoned for only by the shedding of blood, or "Blood Atonement."[5] By this they do not mean sins or transgressions against the civil law, but sins against the Mormon Church and the priestly ordinances. I myself have heard older mothers say in Salt Lake City that they would not hesitate to perform this bloodshed in the case of their own offspring, if they fell away or denied the faith, since this was the only way of salvation for them.

The unbounded power and influence Brigham exerts over the Mormon people becomes understandable when one takes into consideration, along with his all-embracing "religious authority," the enormous revenues which stand at his disposal. Besides the real estate which he has managed to take into his personal possession [p. 38] all over the Territory, he receives and administers all the revenues of the Church. These could be allocated in the following way:

1. "The Continual Immigration Fund," which in part comes from the free-will offerings to the Church, which then loans them to indigent Mormons who want to travel from Europe to Salt Lake City.

2. "The Temple Fund," which also consists of free-will gifts from the "saints" all over the land. I know one Dane who by himself gave 1800 kroner to this fund.

3. "Tithes," which can be subdivided into:

   (a) tenth portions from all property which in case of sale is assessed in cash value (in 1857 Denmark contributed 20,000 kroner to this fund)

   (b) tenth portions of all that which is brought in from agriculture or livestock or likewise all income from industry or the earnings from commercial businesses

   (c) tenth portions from time periods, that is, the work of every ten-day period or its equivalent, on the part of those who earn their living as day laborers or as service personnel or who have

---

5. Murder, adultery, stealing, apostasy, and marrying a Negro were all said to be acts worthy of death. For information concerning blood atonement see *Mormonism: Shadow or Reality?* pp. 398-404.

nothing to do. This last is allowed in order to pay
their tax to the Church by helping to perform the
public work projects of the Church, such as the
erection of meetinghouses, tithe-houses and temples, canals, highways, fortresses, and the like.

Therefore a vast number of work projects are carried
out in Salt Lake upon enterprises of apparently little or no
usefulness, except that they keep the people at work. For
example: the rampart twelve feet high and six feet thick,
complete with bastions and crenelations, which was to
encircle Salt Lake City and was calculated to cover an
area of six English square miles. Likewise the eight-mile
canal which was dug out between the city and Cotton-
wood River, by which stone was to be conveyed for the
new temple by canal boats instead of by land, as now is
done.

How Brigham Young, as the legal representative and
plenipotentiary (Trustee in trust) of the Mormon society,
carries on government and gives account for his adminis-
tration of the affairs of the Church may be seen by the
following information from a trustworthy source. In 1852
he adjusted his little deficit to the Church, in the amount of
$200,000, by having [p. 39] his bookkeepers enter in the
sum of $200,000 for "services rendered" by Brigham
Young, and in 1867 he determined his worth to the Church
at the amount of $967,000 by a similar method. It really
does not require any miracle to remain a "big man," when
one has such sources of help in a land where crime is only
accounted as such in cases where the criminal is a wretch
who lacks the required cash.

Just as little as the Church as a whole is the individual
citizen so completely secure in his private property in
Utah. Joseph Smith already attempted to introduce a kind
of communism under the name of "Enoch's Order" among
the Mormons in order to bind them more firmly together,
but the plan met with opposition and did not come into
operation in his time. In recent years Brigham Young has
brought "Enoch's Order" back into consideration and
made this precise theme the burning question for the present day in Utah. Whoever goes into Enoch's Order must
convey his entire property by a legally worded document
to Brigham Young as "trustee in trust" for the "The
Church of Jesus Christ of the Latter Day Saints." Thereby

he of course takes control over all the landed properties and can, if the owners should become fed up with Brigham Young's paternal government and feel a desire to leave his realm, let them go naked and empty-handed. Brigham, who has for a long time lived in luxury and abundance, knows very well the weakness of men over against "the world and all that is in the world." When he tells the "faithful" "after we tether the calf, the cow does not run away!" then they smile broadly at his cleverness and are happy at the thought of how the faithless "apostates" will get into a tight spot. The poor, misled fools never stop to think that they are at the same time selling and giving away their own freedom and that of their children.

Even in regard to the faithful, the Church and the Prophet sometimes do not conduct themselves quite honorably in financial matters, as the reader will see from a few examples.

In 1852 a lady named Fresne migrated from the island of Jersey to Utah. At her departure she had more money than necessary for the journey, and she therefore offered the Church [p. 40] a loan of $2,500 for six months. The money was accepted with gratitude, and S. W. Richards, the agent of the Church in Liverpool, England, signed a pledge for repayment and a promissory note or bill of exchange drawn on Brigham Young for the specified sum. Upon her arrival in Salt Lake City the old lady presented the bill of exchange in the belief that the money would be repaid her with as great a willingness as she had lent it to them, but she was bitterly disappointed in this. The bill was neither acknowledged nor repaid, and when she requested an explanation, she was informed that she could take a city lot with an old house on it; if she was not satisfied with that, she would get nothing. The lady registered objections, and they just laughed at her. She put up an argument, and she was met with a mandate. She became angry and was kicked out onto the street. She left Salt Lake City and traveled to California without a single shilling or any hope that her loss would be made up.

By the personal influence of the apostle John Taylor some well-to-do Englishmen were moved to collect a capital of $100,000 for the purchase of machines, and so on, for eventual clothing factories and sugar factories in Salt

Lake City. They believed the Apostle's promises and forgot all about specifying conditions about progress or profit, not only because they regarded him as an honorable man, but first and foremost because he was one of their own holy apostles. The sanguine and gullible "saints" bought machines, sheep, sugar-beet seed, and such like, and journeyed off with it; but upon arrival in St. Louis one of them became aware of John Taylor's real character and motives. He abandoned Mormonism and journeyed back to his business in Liverpool, while his erstwhile companions continued the trip to Salt Lake City, where Brigham Young* took over the machines and everything else without further ado.

*The original text reads "B. Y." —Ed.

Mr. Delamere, one of the victims who was robbed and ruined finally had to make his living by laboring at a smithy. Another, named Coward, had to make his living by chopping firewood on the mountains, until his health was ruined. And Russell, the third victim, died so suddenly [p. 41] that the Church found it to its advantage to appoint itself as administrator and take permanent possession of his residence. One of Brigham Young's missionaries in England named Cyrup Wheelock had borrowed a large sum of money from a Mr. Lee from Lancastershire in England, with the promise to repay it after his return home to Zion. Then when Lee had fortunately returned home with "saints of the Lord" in order to "sit under his own fig tree," etc., he addressed himself to him in the presence of the loving "brothers of Zion," the "servants of the Lord," and so on, in order to get his money back. But Wheelock responded to him with the following characteristically cool reply: "I have given the money to the poor saints. I am not going to pay it back and what can you do about it?" Like all the other fools, Lee naturally went to Brigham Young, in order that this infallible judge, who leaves no sinner unpunished, might get him his money back again. But instead of that he received the following ruling from the Prophet: "If an elder borrows money from you, and you find that he is in the process of forsaking the faith, then you can put the screws on him. But so long as he is ready to preach the Gospel without purse or money pouch, then it is not up to you how he uses the money he borrows from you. The Lord wants money for them to spend; let it go and don't be concerned how he spends it. If you raise a

complaint against this elder, it will be to your own con-
demnation. The money is not yours, but the Almighty gave
it into your hands to see what you would do with it."

In reality Mormon doctrine itself is stripped of all Christian morality; it has only the one great commandment:
"blind, unconditional obedience" to the Prophet and the
leaders of the Church.[6] Its faith and works which Christian
doctrine presupposes have nothing to do with each other—
as can be seen from the following speech which Brigham
Young gave concerning his predecessor, Joseph Smith.
"The doctrine he proclaimed," says the Prophet, "is completely what I am saying. Above and beyond anything
against him, if you know of it—I am not in the least concerned if in other matters he may have acted like [p. 42] a
devil. He has set forth a teaching which will save us if we
abide in it. He may even have gotten drunk every single
day of his life, or slept with his neighbor's wife every single
night, made bets or indulged in gambling. I am not at all
concerned about that, for I never include any human being in my faith. The teaching he has brought forth will save
you and me and the whole world.—If you find anything
wrong with that, then do so!" (Cf. *Deseret News*, December
18, 1856.) This was certainly encouraging to hear from
"the Lord's anointed" about his forerunner Joseph Smith,
whom the Lord had raised up in these last days in order to
establish His kingdom once more, and His Church upon
earth. Christendom may have gone storming ahead into
liberalism since the days of the Savior and the Apostles,
because in those days men believed that "God was holy" in
such a way that nothing unclean could enter into His
realm, and that the Holy Spirit would not dwell in impure
temples—"If ye believe not My word, then believe in Me
for My work's sake!" said Christ.—But the new Prophet
can readily "sleep with his neighbor's wife," "get drunk
every day," "play games of chance," etc. What is that to us?
"Who can say anything against his teaching?" asks
Brigham triumphantly. In all humility we would cite the
Bible's answer to that: "Can anyone gather grapes from
thorns or figs from thistles? Can the same spring yield both
sweet and bitter water?"

---

6. Heber Kimball admonished the Mormon people to "learn to do as you
   are told . . . if you are told by your leader to do a thing, do it, none of
   your business whether it is right or wrong" (*Journal of Discourses*,
   6:32).

This in short was how I found Mormonism in Utah. This is the way it leads this people in respect to morality, people whose industry and perseverance must be admired, but at the same time whose destiny we must deplore which they all too unthinkingly are going to meet.

It was my decision to leave Utah in company with several compatriots and go to California early in the following year, but because of the fearsome threats which were constantly uttered in the Tabernacle and the meetinghouses against "apostates and heathen" from then on like an echo from mouth to mouth among the people,[7] our decision was altered and we determined to travel back to the eastern States in company with [p. 43] the larger groups that were gathered in Salt Lake City and organized for mutual security.

The US Judge Drummond had already traveled from Utah in May, and General Burr with the rest of the US officials and a crowd of "apostates and heathen" departed in April. And so I secured passage for myself and my family with a merchant train belonging to a Mr. Fernandes from Weston, Missouri, which consisted of eighteen wagons, each of which was drawn by eight oxen. On the eighteenth of April, 1857, I left great Salt Lake City after a four months' sojourn in it, and the following day we set up camp at the Big and Little Mountains. Here we joined up with a larger company of emigrants who likewise had seen enough of the "promised land," and whose hearts already, like the new spring, seemed to breathe new life and new hope. From the summit of the great mountain which we reached on the following day, we saw the last of Zion and all its glories, and we now proceeded once more through the huge mountain masses whose snow-capped summits seemed all cloaked about for reaching up to the sky. The atmosphere was rarified and cold, for although the snow had melted on the west side of the mountain, it still lay in heavy masses on the east side, which we could climb over only by morning, during which the icy crust could still bear up under the large, heavily laden wagons. It took us two days to get over the big mountain. Twelve or fifteen yoke of oxen often enough have all they can do to pull one

---

7. Brigham Young stated, "I say, rather than the apostates should flourish here, I will unsheath my bowie knife, and conquer and die" (*Journal of Discourses*, 1:83). For other warnings and threats issued against apostates see *Journal of Discourses*, 4:219-20; 6:34-35.

of the wagons up the mountain, and the descent is even worse, for the crust breaks and the wagons sink down. Thus we would come to a complete stop, or else the heavy wagon might commence to slide down by itself and—then God help anything that gets in the way! After the descent was accomplished one feels light of heart and marvels that "things went as fortunately as they did!"—So at one time we could proceed on between the cold masses of snow up on the mountains and the next hour come down into a narrow snow-covered valley where trees, flowers, and grass spread their charm and fragrance. On the twenty-seventh of July we finally reached the city of Leavenworth, Kansas, ready to begin living a new life again, with a sincere desire to see once more the charming, fertile islands of Denmark.

5 Polygamy Among the Mormons

[p. 44] It is said that already in 1838 Joseph Smith had received his first revelation concerning the system of polygamy and practiced it at the same time.[1] Yet in a revelation to His "servant Joseph" in 1831 He had said: "Thou shalt love thy wife with all thy heart and keep thyself for her alone." In 1842 it was rumored that in Nauvoo plural marriage was an article of faith in Mormonism, but the elders of the Church publicly countered[2] this rumor with the following explanation, which was established as an addition to the "Doctrines of the Church and the Book of the Covenant": "Whereas this church has been blamed for practicing loose living and polygamy, it is explained by the fact that according to our belief a man is to have one wife, and a wife only one husband, except in the case of death, where the survivor has the freedom to get married again."

---

1. Actually, Joseph Smith gave a revelation concerning polygamy in 1831. According to Mormon historian Hyrum Andrus, "The Prophet understood the principle of plural marriage as early as 1831" (*Doctrines of the Kingdom* (Salt Lake City: Bookcraft, 1973, p. 450). It is interesting that according to this revelation Mormon men were to marry Indians to make them white (see Leonard J. Arrington and Davis Bitton, *The Mormon Experience* (New York: Knopf, 1979), p. 195.
2. See p. 14 (of the Danish work).

At the same time these elders surely knew that Joseph Smith had living children by several wives. Parley P. Pratt, the first and most respected of the twelve Apostles refuted the same accusation in a speech which he gave in a general conference of the Mormon church in Manchester, England: "Such a teaching," he said, "is neither known, believed or practiced by the Latter Day Saints. Polygamy is just another name for harlotry and is just as far removed from the operative principle of this church as Satan is from God" (cf. *Millennial Star*, volume 6, page 2).

John Taylor—also one of the most respected apostles and an eyewitness of the murder of Joseph Smith in Carthage jail—countered the same accusation as [p. 45] he worked for the Mormon propaganda agency in 1850 in Boulogne, France. There Taylor was challenged by another clergyman to a public debate, which he afterwards had printed and distributed among the European missions. It went as follows: "We are accused of polygamy and of actions of such an indecent and abhorrent character as no one but the most depraved could have invented. These things are too gross to be believed. I shall therefore restrict myself to reading to you a few excerpts from our scriptures which discuss our views concerning the marital state." He reads from the "Book of the Covenant," page 311: "You are both united so as to be marriage partners to each other, man and wife, and so as to respect all the legal obligations which this relationship involves. That is to say: you will keep yourselves entirely for each other and from anyone else for your entire life!" And on the same page: "Inasmuch as the Church of Jesus Christ has been accused of loose living and polygamy, we hereby declare that according to our belief a man is to have one wife and wife only one husband. . . !" Likewise on page 224: "Thou shalt love thy wife with all thine heart and keep thyself for her alone. He who looks upon a woman to lust after her shall be cast out, for he denies the faith and does not have the Spirit." "These are our teachings concerning this point," John Taylor exclaimed with great unction; but at the same time this apostle had actually four wives in Utah and was making negotiations for a fifth in the Island of Jersey.[a3]

---

a. Cf. *Mormonism* by Hyde, as well as Stenhouse's *Rocky Mountain Saints*.

3. This denial of John Taylor's was reprinted in *Orson Pratt's Works* (Liverpool: 1851 edition). The names of the wives that Taylor had at

The Mormons adhered with perfect equanimity to this disgusting, cowardly, mendacious system of denial until Brigham Young in 1852 had a previously granted revelation publicly announced, which Joseph Smith was supposed to have received in Nauvoo in July 1843. To be sure, Brigham states that this teaching had its beginning at that time, but the [p. 46] revelation itself shows that this was a lie.[b] That is to say, it says in paragraph 20: " . . . Let my maidservant, Emma Smith (Joseph's wife) receive all those who are devoted to my servant Joseph, those who are virtuous and pure virgins for me!"—Therefore she was not to receive the "virtuous and pure" virgins who eventually had to be given to him, but those who had already been so given. The reason for the appearance of this vision probably was that principally Joseph had wanted to subdue his wife Emma and if possible move her to go in on the fabrication. She was constantly opposed to her husband's "spiritual marriage doctrine" and was still seriously considering divorce proceedings, as can be clearly seen from the following paragraph of the aforesaid revelation, where he conveys the following friendly warning: "I order my handmaid Emma Smith to remain with and keep herself for My servant Joseph and for no other. But if she will not obey this command, she shall be destroyed," says the Lord, "for I am the Lord thy God, and I will destroy her, if she does not obey and keep My law!" (*Revelation Concerning Polygamy*, paragraph 21).

In a speech Brigham Young delivered during a trip to the southern part of Utah,[c] he related how, among other

this time can be found in B. H. Roberts, *The Life of John Taylor* (Salt Lake City: Bookcraft, 1963), a later edition of the 1892 reprint.

For other public denials of plural marriage see *Messenger and Advocate*, 3:511; *Documentary History of the Church*, 3:28; 5:72; 6:354-55, 4ll; *Times and Seasons*, 5:474, 715; 6:888, 894; *Millennial Star*, 6:22; 12:29-30; *Nauvoo Neighbor*, June 19, 1844 (this last reference was reprinted in the *Documentary History of the Church*, 6:435, with alterations to cover up falsehoods expressed in the public denials as printed in the *Nauvoo Neighbor*). The references cited in this footnote are all available at the Harold B. Lee Library at BYU.

b. The speech was reprinted in one of the first issues of the Dano-Norwegian Newspaper, *Utah Posten*.

c. This document has the following heading: "A Revelation concerning the Patriarchal Marriage Ordinance, or Plurality of Wives. Given to Joseph Smith the Seer in Nauvoo, July 12, 1843." It is composed of twenty-five paragraphs which consistently show the prophet's effort to imitate Jehovah speaking to Moses. It begins, "Verily, thus saith the Lord," and ends with, "Behold I am Alpha and Omega. Amen." (Continued on next page) things, Joseph Smith asked for his (i.e., Brigham's) own sister to be his wife. The girl opposed this and answered [p. 47] his statement that a woman could not be saved or exalted except by such a marriage—that she would rather be a ministering angel in heaven. "Sister," answered the prophet, "you don't know what you will think when you get there!"—And thus he gave orders to her brother (Brigham) to perform the wedding ceremony for 'time and eternity'!" Nonetheless this tender and sensitive brother comes in 1852 and tells us that now plural marriage begins, [and]* wants to make us believe in these days that "the sisters" in Utah are stronger in their faith in polygamy than "the brethren" are. That is just as kind as the artful claim behind which polygamists in Utah try to cover themselves. Who can doubt that women have to sacrifice their best and purest feelings in such an unnatural marriage state, rather than viewing the matter and feeling that way about it themselves. But in Utah it is first and foremost "to obey!" The fact that Brigham Young's own wives have at this time collected 23,000 women's signatures in a petition to Congress to annul the so-called Poland Law[d] is merely an additional indication of their hopelessly subjugated condition.[4]

*This word added for clarity. —Trans.

The theory on which the Mormons support their polygamy is about as follows. In the preexisting spirit world there is assuredly a number of spirits who are destined to be born on earth. Their presence there as human beings is

---

(Continued from previous page)
Concerning the origin of this "divine" (but for Smith and his adherents a most unfortunate) revelation, Stenhouse relates the following in his account, *The Rocky Mountain Saints:* "The prophet entered his office in the morning, shut the door and became inspired. His amanuensis, Elder William Clayton, now in Salt Lake City, wrote the 'revelation' down as Joseph dictated it to him."

d. A law which establishes a fine of $500 and imprisonment up to five years for polygamy.

---

4. In fact, there was much discord and sorrow among many Utah women concerning polygamy. Heber Kimball once stated, "There is a great deal of quarrelling in the houses, and contending for power and authority; and the second wife is against the first wife, perhaps in some instances" (*Journal of Discourses,* 4:178). Brigham Young himself stated, "A few years ago one of my wives when talking about wives leaving their husbands said, 'I wish my husband's wives would leave him, every soul of them except myself.' That is the way they all feel, more or less, at times both young and old" (*Journal of Discourses,* 9:195).

a necessary place of transition for them to attain the greatest perfection in the future world. But since these are elect
spirits, they must also have specially chosen bodies to give
them life down here. And for this reason the Mormons are
very zealous to bring forth "a pure and chosen seed" by
the aid of heavenly marriage (sealings). Furthermore the
Mormons are going to reign in the future world as "kings
and priests," etc. But it is well to note that it will be only
over their own family, and so the more wives and children
[p. 48] a Mormon can come by down here, the greater are
his prospects for his future "kingdoms." Those who do not
take part in the heavenly marriages of New Zion can attain
to no better than the status of servant personnel in heaven.
"In heaven there will also be some usefulness for shoe-
blacks," says Brigham.[5]

When looked at from a worldly standpoint, the idea of
plural marriage may have some attractiveness and appeal
for certain men. That is to say, if one imagines himself to
be a Muslim or a Turk walking around in splendid harems,
surrounded by semiveiled beauties, while a soft, delightful
music is heard and pervasive fragrances excite the senses,
then the picture is quite fascinating. But in actual practice
it looks quite different.

Let one kindly imagine himself to be a poor homeowner,
for example, in his meager and occasionally dirty surroundings, with five or six half-naked wives and various
groups of hungry children moved by envy and mistrust for
one another. Let him consider whether this isn't a bit less
desirable than domestic love and comfort; then the picture
becomes completely repellent and unpleasant. Brigham
Young himself has had a little example along this line. His
nineteenth wife, Anna Elisabeth, applied to the courts for
a divorce from the prophet on grounds of neglect of his
duties toward her and complete abandonment of her over
a lengthy period of time, etc. She requested also annual
financial support in proportion to her husband's income.
Brigham responded to this under oath that "Anna Elisabeth neither was his wife nor ever had been," and that he
had "only one wife, Mary A. Angel, who was wed to him in

---

5. At another time Young stated, "The only men who become Gods, even
   the sons of God, are those who enter into polygamy" (*Journal of Discourses*, 11:269).

Kirtland, Ohio, on January 10, 1834."[e] Anna Elisabeth on her part testified in court that she had been married to Brigham Young since April 6, 1868, but that he had abandoned her and contributed nothing to her support since the fall of [p. 49] 1873, even though he possessed several million dollars.

Eventually the prophet explained that he had actually got married to Anna Elizabeth,* but she had only been his "spiritual wife according to Mormon religious law," etc. In regard to the millions of dollars, he maintained that his income at the most amounted to "$40,000 a month"! The court ruled that the prophet had to pay court costs plus $9,500 to Anna Elizabeth.[f] On the twenty-first of September 1856, Brigham Young gave a short speech in the Tabernacle that characterizes the family life of polygamists so nicely, and we cite the following quote which was printed in the chief news organ of the Church, *Deseret News:*

The spelling difference in the name "Elizabeth" here (z instead of s as on p. 48) is in the original Danish. —Trans.

> . . . Now to my proposition which pertains to the sisters, since it often happens that they complain and say that they are unfortunate, there are also men who say, "My wife has not had a happy time since I took my second wife." "No, not a single happy day in a year!"—says one; and again another says: "My wife has not seen a happy day in five years." That means that the woman is oppressed and mistreated, that such women do not enjoy [p. 50] the freedom they should— yes, that many of them go through a veritable flood of tears because of their own husband's behavior in connection with their own follies. I want my own wives to understand that I

e. This declaration of Brigham's is very significant and it shows up Mormonism in its true light. As a prophet he explains to the "saints" that plural marriage is a "divine revelation" and "mandate," etc., and that civil marriage within the temporal law is of little value by comparison with the other. But when the prophet stands before an earthly bar of judgment he displays the other side of the picture. Here he wants his civil marriage with his first wife, Mrs. Angel, to be recognized as the exclusively valid one, even though he thereby, just to save himself a paltry sum of money, betrays his own wives along with two-thirds of the married population of Utah and declares their marital situation to be unlawful—so that these credulous wives and those children of theirs whom he himself had sealed with "the sacred authority of the priesthood"—"for time and eternity"—are now without the rights of the married status or protection! A wonderful prophet and servant of the Lord he is in very truth!

f. She had not yet received this sum. Brigham refuses to pay, and since Judge McKean had him arrested in this case, the US government had him deposed as judge!—So it goes in America!

talk to them as much as I do to others. I want those of them who are here present to say to their sisters, or indeed, to every woman in this society and after that send it out by letter throughout the United States! Do whatever you want with this: from now until the sixth of October I am giving you time to think it over whether you want to stay with your husband or not. Even so I give all women free choice and say to them, "Go your way, now—my own along with the rest—go your way!" And my wives have to do one of two things—either bend their backs and endure the difficulties of this world and live according to their religion—or go away—for I will not have them near me. I would rather go to heaven by myself than have strife and dissension around me. I give them all their freedom! "How is that! Even your first wife too?"—"Yes, I free them all." I know my wives will say, yes, they would say: "You can take just as many wives as you want, Brigham!" But I want to go somewhere to get rid of these nuisances![g]

When Brigham Young finds it necessary to use such language concerning his own family situation that he knows about, what are we to think of polygamy on the part of the poor and simple social class? Divorces naturally belong to the order of the day in Utah.[6] Elder John Hyde says that he knew a woman who went through six divorces, and he cites several examples of people who have sought divorces two or three days after their marriage. Brigham alone has the authority to seal and dissolve these "celestial" marriages, and this is not his least lucrative business. A sealing for "time" costs $10; if it is to be for "all eternity" [p. 51] the party concerned has to lay out $50. Under ordinary circumstances Brigham is apparently liberal in regard to time payments, but in 1854, when divorces reached epidemic proportions in Utah, it is expressly affirmed that the prophet required spot cash[h] that in this way particularly he might put a stop to the mounting divorce rate.

Since Moses' time at least all civilized or even half-civilized nations have forbidden marriage between members

g. Cf. *Deseret News*, October 1, 1856.

h. Money was at that time almost unknown in Utah. All business and trade took place by the medium of barter of every type of product, and even tickets to Brigham's theater were paid for in kind.

6. Utah divorce rates have been above the national average in recent years.

of the same family, but that doesn't phase the Mormons. The Prophet is so far from offering objection to sealing a man to two or three natural sisters at one time that on the contrary he recommended it as a good idea, in order to obviate strife in respect to superior position in the family. Examples are also found of a man married to and living with both mother and daughter at the same time.[7]

The reason for the appearance of plural marriage among the Mormons must undoubtedly be looked for in Joseph Smith's very sensual disposition. The Book of Mormon and the Book of the Covenant clearly testify that he had no thought of it at the beginning of his prophetic career. For example, in the Book of Mormon David and Solomon are condemned because of their many "wives and concubines"—which the Lord at that time declared to be "an abomination." Out of all the misleading sophistries which the Mormons have hit upon in order to defend polygamy, only one has any logic to it, considered from their standpoint. The Mormons, who seek to establish an independent earthly power, see the necessity of a rapid increase in numbers in order to attain this desired result. By preaching the "everlasting gospel" Joseph Smith converted 100,000 proselytes in a surprisingly short time, but when they learned to know the prophet and his teaching more closely, dissatisfaction and defection arose. [p. 52] The Americans became wary of its harmfulness and the existence of "the Kingdom" was threatened. Brigham had to move the "kingdom" of Zion off to the mountain cliffs and saw himself principally directed to bring in proselytes from Great Britain and the Scandinavian countries; but this increase was slow and costly in relationship to the great amount of falsehoods, money, human lives, and strenuous exertions which it cost him. Plural marriage is, on the other hand, a much cheaper way to obtain subjects. It only requires continued effort and supremacy among the leaders of Utah to subdue and get rid of the "old traditions" of the Bible, which often evoked disturbing symptoms among the older proselytes. For this reason Brigham

7. Historian Fawn Brodie has pointed out that Joseph Smith himself married five pairs of sisters: Delcena and Almera Johnson, Eliza and Emily Partridge, Sarah and Maria Lawrence, Mary Ann and Olive Grey Frost, and Prescinda and Zina Huntington. Patty and Sylvia Sessions, two other of Smith's wives, were mother and daughter. See *No Man Knows My History* (New York: Knopf, 1957), p. 336.

Young transformed the teaching of polygamy from a "Satanic lie" into a divine truth.—When a man can get five
children from one wife, the same man with nineteen wives
can get ninety-five, or an increase of ninety subjects without costing the Church one cent. That is profitable, says
Brigham Young—not only does it afford good prospects
for the future greatness of the kingdom, but also for the
future existence of the Mormon realm among the mountain cliffs. For these children of a "chosen seed" would not
be troubled by old traditions but would increase and progress in the faith in such splendid institutions as polygamy,
the Danites and the Endowment, and so on, which the
prophet sees in his spirit!

That He who in the beginning created man as husband
and wife and ordained that the two should "be one flesh,"
did not appoint such a relationship between the two sexes
as polygamy presupposes, seems further confirmed by the
results that nature's own law affords in this direction.
From the population figures given for the Mormons in
Utah in 1851 we find that there were 6,020 males and only
5,310 females—therefore 710 less than the male population. Now when an old polygamist like Young, et al., has
from three to twenty wives, it is obvious that their "brothers" are thereby deprived. In the US census of 1850 the
entire number of those born is found to yield a total of
19,553,068. Of these 10, 026,377 were boys and 9,526,691
were girls; [p. 53] therefore the male children were almost 500,000 in the majority. According to the census in
England of 1851, including a time-span of fifty years, the
proportion of births of the two sexes revealed itself to be
105 to 97.5; and in Scotland over the same period there
was a similar imbalance between the two genders, namely
84 to 73. In Prussia the relationship between the two sexes
in 1849 stood as follows: 8,162,805 males, and 8,162,382
females. Thus plural marriage, both in theory and in practice, is an unnatural condition and a false unnatural doctrine which is rightly labeled "a remnant of the barbarism
of earlier times!"

6 The Prophet Morris

"Freedom of conscience and of faith" has always been the watchcry of Mormonism when it makes its entrance among those of other faiths and of foreign countries. Its attack has always been sustained against every other denomination on the ground of the "unchristian" intolerance with which it opposes Brigham's apostles. Now let us look for just a moment at how Christian toleration is practiced in "Zion," and how great a measure of freedom of conscience and of faith is discoverable among the Latter Day Saints. The prophet Morris and the fate of his adherents afford us an uncommonly clear and telling illustration in this regard.

In 1862 there arose in Utah a new prophet [p. 54] by the name of Joseph Morris. He maintained that the Lord had sent him to "redeem Israel," which had fallen into sin and ungodliness under the regime of Brigham Young. The numerous adherents whom Morris had gradually drawn to himself he gathered into a colony at the so-called Fort Kingston by the Weber River, about thirty-five miles north of Salt Lake City. Here he erected a new Zion whose members stood under certain special regulations, such as community of property, for example, and so on. People came streaming to him from all the districts of Utah and testified that they were fed up with Brigham Young's government.

In his colony Morris continued to receive a great many revelations, among which was one for Brigham Young, whom the Lord admonished, threatened, rebuked, and so on. But the new prophet's most important revelation, however, consisted of a message that Christ's return to reign upon earth was close at hand. Among many other zany ideas he had also hit upon the notion that the foremost of his followers had lived on earth with different names, like "Enoch," "Elijah," "Esther," and so on. He kept no less than six secretaries busy, three English and three Danish, with the writing down of his revelations.

But after one week passed, and then another, and Christ still did not come to earth, a schism arose among the "elect" beside the Weber River. Some apostates wanted to leave the colony, but now the question concerning the division of property came up. It ended up with the "apostates" trying to assert their own rights, and after that, three of them were arrested by the Morrisites. The families and friends of the prisoners applied to the authorities in the Weber District to effect their release, and when the authorities in question could accomplish nothing, they went to Brigham Young, and from him to the US judge in Utah, whose name was Kinney and who was known for his friendly attitude toward the Mormons. The judge then issued a writ of *habeas corpus*, or an order to release the prisoners, and he sent the territorial marshal to serve it on Morris; but the marshal had to return home with the mission unaccomplished. Shortly after that the judge issued a new order, which had just as little effect upon [p. 55] the errant, fanatical Morrisites, who fully expected that the Lord was coming down from heaven with "His many thousands" in order to annihilate their enemies completely. Kinney became angry at this resistance, and he requisitioned a substantial military force to accompany the marshal on his third trip there, and if necessary, to carry out the order by force.

On June 3, early in the morning, the detachment of troops reached the Weber River and took up positions on a height which commanded the encampment of the Morrisites. By one of the Morrisites' shepherd boys the following proclamation was sent:

Marshall's Headquarters
Weber River, June 13, 1862

To Joseph Morris, John Banks, Richard Cook,
J. Parson and John Klemgaard!

Inasmuch as you have hitherto despised and rejected the
law of your Territory and its appointed officials; and inasmuch as certain legal decrees were issued to you from the
judicial court in the third administrative district, and an
appropriate military force has been sent to support the authority of the law, therefore we order you forthwith and
without resistance to surrender yourselves and your prisoners into our hands. If we do not receive an answer within
thirty minutes after that you have received this document,
you will become subject to arrest by force. Should you put
your lives in jeopardy by rejecting this proposal, let your
wives and children and any other peace-minded person depart from your encampment without delay. They will find
protection with us.

K. W. Lawrence, Marshall, Utah Territory
R. T. Burton, Theodore McKean, Deputies

When the Morrisites received this document, the question arose as to what they should do. The prophet answered that he would go and "inquire of the Lord." At the
same time the people assembled in their meeting place
and after they had a brief time of prayer, the prophet
entered with a written revelation in his hand. In this revelation, which was read aloud by John Parsons, the Lord
said [p. 56] that He had brought the soldiers against His
chosen ones, the Morrisites, in order that by the total
destruction of their enemies they might make His power
known. The chosen ones were now to triumph over their
enemies without disturbing a hair on their heads.

Thereupon Richard Cook stood up and put the question
before the people whether it was best to obey the marshall
or to obey the revelation of the Lord. They considered the
matter, but thirty minutes was soon up, and before the
poor, misguided people had come to a decision a shot rang
out and a cannonball landed in the meetinghouse, killed
two women, and tore the undergarments of one little girl.
Shot followed upon shot, and the marshall's troops came
closer and closer to the camp, in which the most fearful
confusion prevailed. At the first shock of terror everyone

tried to escape the best way he could, but when they returned to their senses, the Morrisites quickly took their wives and children to a place of safety and then defended themselves with weapons in hand for three days with considerable courage.

Morris was receiving revelations by the bushel: "The hosts of darkness that fought against the Lamb and His armies" were too high-handed for the time being; the unbelief of God's own people and their transgressions were too great—and these circumstances would delay the coming of Christ, etc. The people fasted and prayed and clothed themselves in pure, white raiment, and they stood in complete expectation of seeing Christ come down in power and glory from heaven to deliver them.

After waiting in vain for three days they finally decided to surrender to the marshall, and for that purpose they raised a white flag. Thereupon Colonel Burton approached the camp for a cautious reconnoiter with a detachment of soldiers, and what took place after that is relayed by an eyewitness under oath, Alexander Dow, as follows:

> . . . Robert Burton and Judson I. Stoddard rode in among the Morrisites. Burton was very quick-tempered and cried out angrily, "Where is the man? I don't know him!" Stoddard pointed at Morris and answered, "He's the one." Burton, who was on horseback, went up to Morris and ordered him to surrender. "No, never, never!" answered Morris and indicated that he wanted to speak to the people. [p. 57] "Be done with it [_____] fast!" yelled Burton. "Brethren," Morris began, "I have taught you principles of truth . . ." These words were scarcely out of his mouth before Burton fired his revolver. The shot struck Morris in the back of the neck and in one shoulder. "There is your prophet!" cried Burton and at the same time fired another shot, saying, "What do you think of your prophet now?" Then he wheeled his horse around and shot Banks, who was standing about five or six paces away. As Banks fell, the wife of James Bowman came running up and cried out, "Oh you bloodthirsty wretch!" Burton yelled back, "No one can say that to me and live!" and he shot her. A Danish woman ran up solicitously to Morris and tried to assist him; Burton killed her also with a pistol shot. He could very easily have taken Morris and Banks prisoner if that had been his purpose.—Alexander Dow

—Testified under oath before me, April 18, 1863
—Charles B. Waite, Judge Utah Territory.

During the siege two of Burton's soldiers had fallen. The
Morrisites had six dead and three wounded. As already
said, the first cannon shot killed two women and wounded
one girl. Another shot killed a woman and her child. The
prophet's mother-in-law was killed in her cottage, and so
on. The captured Morrisites were taken to Salt Lake City
and came up for a hearing before the aforementioned
Judge Kinney. Five of the community were indicted for
murder, sixty-six of them for insurrection against the lawful authority. There was nothing said about individual
process of law; there were two prosecutors and two
judges—for eighty-one men!

The five were condemned to prison for six to sixteen
years, which in Utah meant hard labor in chains, working
on Brigham's highway project under the supervision of
Brigham's brother-in-law. The sixty-six were fined $100
apiece, which incidentally was more than any of them
possessed or could come by.

[p. 58] When this drama was over, Brigham was in absolute power in Utah, even though he was no longer Governor. With the exception of the Supreme Court, all executive power was in the hands of the Mormons, and Kinney
was so far from causing difficulties that he was contrari-
wise ready at all times to act as helper and carry out the
wishes of Brigham Young—which was precisely what happened in the present case.

In the meantime Utah's new governer, S. S. Harding,
arrived, and likewise a new Supreme Court justice and a
substantial military contingent under the command of the
famous General Connor. And it was the humaneness of this
gentleman that the harried and hounded Morrisites had to
thank for their release, which they all received shortly
afterward, along with the timely assistance which was
granted them on the part of the government and soon
made their fate more tolerable.

For the time being it did not go so easily for them, for
Brigham had determined completely to subdue and destroy the unfortunate Morrisites. But Governor Harding,
after he had been told of the distress and misery which still
prevailed even among the Morrisites who were not condemned said of them:

. . . Soon after my arrival in the Territory many of these unfortunate men came to me with reproachful tears in their eyes as if I permitted this misfortune which had come upon them. Many of them were from Denmark, and the poor souls seemed to think that a governor was a person who ought to have the same rights and powers as a king in their native land!

A petition was circulated for a pardon to be granted to the Morrisites, and it was signed by the two judges, the military of the United States, and in general by all the "Gentiles"[a] but not by a single Mormon with the exception—very significantly—of the notorious Danite leader, Bill Hickman.

[p. 59] In regard to this matter Governor Harding writes in a letter from Milan, Indiana, on December 23, 1871:

On the third of March, 1863, a large mass meeting was held under the leadership of Brigham Young in which I and the two judges, Waite and Drake, were requested to leave the Territory immediately. On the evening of the sixth Bill Hickman came to my home and stayed until far into the night. He assured me that he was opposed to—and even condemned—the proceedings of the mass meeting, and that he at the same time was personally friendly disposed to me, etc. Naturally I had no great faith in what he was saying, since I knew that Hickman was an eminent Mormon against whom I had never heard a word from any of the leaders of the Church. He expressed himself sharply in regard to the cruelty which had been shown toward the Morrisites. But although his humaneness naturally pleased me, I could hardly fit these expressions of opinion with what I had heard of his previous bloody exploits. He gave me a description of his life and didn't seem to be particularly proud of his title as "captain of the Danites," nor did he express himself otherwise concerning the activities of the Danites. I asked him how he dared to risk expressing such opinions clearly against the wishes of Brigham Young. At the term "risk" the blood seemed to rise to his head; he stopped me as I was speaking, got up and said, "Governor, are you asking how I dare to risk doing something that displeases Brigham Young? I know Brigham Young and his rabbit tracks! Am I

---

a. The Mormons call everyone who does not belong to the Mormon Society a Gentile and a heathen.

afraid of Brigham Young? Governor, Brigham Young has more reason to fear Bill Hickman than Bill Hickman has to fear Brigham Young!"

The governor said:

> I have never seen a face which expressed more defiance and contempt . . . The wives and mothers of the condemned Morrisites came to me by the dozen and begged me on bended knees with tears in their eyes to show compassion toward their husbands and sons. At the same time baleful threats were directed at me by the Mormon partisans if I should show them any favor. Bishop Wolley tried to scare me by the observation that he would not be [p. 60] responsible for my personal safety if I pardoned these men. Finally the petition for a pardon was presented before me; this happened rather late in the evening, and so it could not be put into effect before the next day. When I had gone to bed and had just fallen asleep, I heard a voice outside calling for the governor. My son went downstairs with the always indispensable revolver in his hand and asked who its was. "Bill Hickman!" was the reply, "Let me come in!" Upon his entrace he asked, "Governor, didn't you think that Brigham Young had sent emissaries after you? When you heard my voice, weren't you afraid?" "Oh no, not very much," I answered. "Governor," he exclaimed, "I can rely on you and you can rely on me!" Then he told me that he had lain awake overnight thinking about the pardon petition, and so at last he got up and rode fourteen miles to come to me and sign the petition himself. He asked me whether any Mormon had signed it. When I answered him, "No," he asked for the document and then took out a pen and wrote across it with big letters like Hancock's signature upon the Declaration of Independence: "Bill Hickman" "There!" he said with great self-satisfaction and pushed the paper aside "Now he can do what he wants about it. Yet there is a Mormon who dares to do according to his own mind in spite of him."[b]

The day after the Governor issued the order for a pardon, and the condemned Morrisites were reunited with their homeless families. But neither the Governor nor the Morrisites would have gotten away with it so easily had it not been for General Connor's soldiers and a few mortars

---

b. See Governor Harding's letter to I. G. Beadle, Esq., December 23, 1871; Hickman's Confession, note K.

from Fort Douglas which could rake the prophet's garden-house with fire—these kept the prophet within the traces, so to speak.

The facts adduced above afford a clear and plain picture, as stated, concerning the freedom of faith and conscience [p. 61] which the Mormons enjoy. Brigham Young had no particular reason to fear a fanatical enthusiast like Joseph Morris. He along with his adherents had lived in hopes for the soon arrival of Christ, and for that reason they had given up all concern about sustenance for the future. They did not sow and they did not reap; consequently the little that they had brought along in the way of provisions to their encampment was soon consumed, and the movement would most likely have come to an end right there. But Mormonism was thirsting for blood; and Brigham tolerates no rivals in his prophetic office. He is very tolerant in regard to which invisible gods his subjects believe in and worship; but woe to the wretch who believes in any other prophet! "Allah is great!" said Mohammed. "The prophet is greater," says Brigham Young.[1]

---

1. For a thorough study of the Morris affair, see C. Leroy Anderson, *For Christ Will Come Tomorrow: The Saga of the Morrisites* (Logan, Utah: USU Press, 1982). The affair is also dealt with in Stenhouse's *Rocky Mountain Saints*, chap. 51 (available at Utah Lighthouse Ministry, Salt Lake City). The incident from a Mormon perspective is found in the *Comprehensive History of the Church*, 5:39-60.

7 The Book of Mormon

Orson Pratt, one of the best Mormon writers and most respected apostles, expresses himself concerning the Book of Mormon in the following manner: "The message of the Book of Mormon is of such a nature that if it is true, no one can be saved who rejects it; and if it is false, no one can be saved who accepts it." We would add that if Joseph Smith's account concerning the appearance of the Book of Mormon is false, then Joseph Smith was a deceiver and Mormonism is a fraud.

Joseph Smith claims that in September 1823 [p. 62] an angel revealed himself to him and told him that the Book of Mormon lay buried in a hill not far from Manchester, in Ontario County, New York State. He went to the spot and found both the Book of Mormon and the Urim and Thummim and the breastplates. But the angel forbade him to take possession of these things. Not until September 1827—an incomprehensible delay!—did he receive the treasured articles from the angel's hands. The Book of Mormon consisted of nothing but gold plates, seven inches broad, eight inches long, and six inches thick. They were fastened together by three rings on one side, and they were covered or written over in a kind of hieroglyphics which no linguist alive could read. Smith called the signs "Reformed Egyptian" and claimed that they related the history of America's first inhabitants, or that composed the original of the Book of Mormon, which numbered five or six hundred closely written pages. But how could a young fellow who had not had even enough schooling to write his own mother tongue understand how to read "Reformed Egyptian?" He himself answers this by saying that it was by means of "God's gift and power" and "by means of Urim and Thummim," a stone set in gold that accompanied the plates and possessed such special characteristics that Joseph Smith knew how to see them and translate by means of them.

In any case one does not talk about any linguistic knowledge when it is a matter of "Reformed Egyptian," something that no living philologist has ever heard of up until now. The translation would have to be done by "God's gift and power" or else by a direct revelation.

Smith, who had now married Emma Hale, was not only ignorant but also very lazy. He had to have a man to write down his translation from the golden plates as well as money to live on while this work was under way; but he found both of them at once by applying his prophetic ingenuity. In his vicinity there lived a rich landowner named Martin Harris, and so the prophet directed to him the following speech: "The Lord has bidden me to ask the first man I meet for five hundred dollars, to help me carry out the work of the Lord and translate the Golden Bible."

[p. 63] Martin Harris, who had successively been a Quaker, a Universalist, a Presbyterian, a Baptist, and a Restorationalist,[1] believed him and paid him the money, became an intimate friend of the prophet, and finally became his secretary. Smith and Harris began to translate the Book of Mormon, but since the Lord had forbidden Smith to show the plates to any man, a curtain was suspended between the prophet and his scribe so that the latter might not see the holy things. Harris, however, was not completely devoid of carnal curiosity, and he soon felt an unquenchable thirst to delight his eyes with sight of the

---

1. Besides having vacillated between a number of denominations before becoming a Mormon, Harris later changed religions eight more times, *Improvement Era* (Salt Lake City, March 1969), p. 63.

golden plates. In order to evade his pestering, Smith finally struck off a page, that is, a piece of paper covered with
strange signs, a copy of a plate. Harris took the paper to a
well known philologist, Professor Anton in New York, and
also related to him where it had been written. The professor was warned by this and finally declared that the whole
thing was a humbug and would not be taken in by it.

Since Harris's trip to New York thus failed to satisfy him
completely, Smith received on March 29, 1829, the following revelation for him:

> Behold I say unto thee, since My servant Martin Harris has
> desired of Me a testimony that thou, Joseph Smith my ser-
> vant, hast taken the plates of which it is said and witnessed
> that thou hast received them from Me—behold, thou shalt
> say this to him: ". . . and I have caused thee to enter into
> a covenant with me that thou shalt not show them (the
> plates) to anyone but to him whom I may command thee
> to . . . Behold, if they do not believe My words, neither will
> they behold thee, My servant Joseph—as if it were possible
> for thee to show them all these things which I have entrust-
> ed to thee! Oh this unbelieving and stiffnecked generation!
> My wrath is kindled against it . . ." And so Harris was denied
> a sight of the plates. And yet in the same revelation (para-
> graph 5, page 149 in the Book of the Covenant) he receives a
> command to speak no more about the matter, except that he
> is to say (to the people): "I have seen them (the plates), they
> were shown to me by the power of God . . ." But if he refuses
> to say this, then he is breaking [p. 64] the covenant which
> he previously made with Me; and behold, he is then con-
> demned.

Therefore it seems that Harris had formerly entered into
a covenant with the Lord that he should lie. Perhaps he has
been hesitating too long while the lie is coming out. Therefore he receives another summons to lie and say, "I have
seen them (the plates)"—at the very same time as the Lord
definitely refuses to let him see them. Not until three
months later did Joseph Smith receive a command from
the Lord to show the plates to Oliver Cowdry, David
Whitmer, and Martin Harris; but these eyewitnesses were
in return to sign a written testimony composed by Joseph
Smith, which is found in the Book of Mormon. What sort
of exhibit this was cannot of course be said with definite-

ness, but notwithstanding this testimonial which was giv-
en concerning it, it still does not seem to have satisfied
Harris, for shortly afterward he stole (at the prompting of
his wife) 118 pages of the translated manuscript with the
thought that if Joseph Smith really had an original, he
would then be in a position to repeat the same material in
another translation, yes even in the very same wording,
since he was translating by "God's gift and power." Harris's
scheme was quite clever indeed, but the young prophet
was not too easy to catch. He immediately (June 1828)
received a new revelation in which the Lord ordered him
to discontinue the translation for a while. "God does not
walk in crooked paths or turn to the right or left," came
the word in the just-mentioned revelation—in which Harris was also called an "ungodly man," and so on. Consequently the translation remained at a standstill until April
17, 1829, when Harris's place as secretary was taken by
Oliver Cowdry. During the intervening nine months Smith
proceeded to consider the situation carefully as to how he
could best get himself out of the fix into which that ungodly man had got him. The result of these reflections was a
revelation he received in May 1829. By it he was forbidden
to translate the stolen section of the book again, since an
even more complete account of what had been contained
in the stolen manuscript had been found in another portion of the plates.

This revelation, which takes up six pages in *The Book
[p. 65] of the Covenant*, is a downright masterpiece of sly,
crafty, clever ingenuity; it testifies clearly enough that the
author was much better acquainted with the "crooked"
paths than he was with the straight. Harris's scheme was
completely frustrated, and the translation was therefore
continued with Oliver Cowdry as secretary.

But not even Oliver Cowdry was completely free of carnal curiosity; he too wanted to see the prophet's "golden
plates." Therefore the Lord sent him through Joseph
Smith the following revelation in April 1829:

> Oliver Cowdry! Verily, verily I say unto thee, as truly as
> the Lord lives who is thy God and thy Redeemer, so truly
> shalt thou receive knowledge of that which thou desirest in
> faith with an upright heart, believing that thou shalt re-
> ceive knowledge of ancient, engraved records from olden

times. . . . Therefore doubt not, for it is God's gift[a] and thou shalt hold it in thine hands and perform wondrous works, and no power shall be able to take it from thine hands, for this is the work of God. And whatever thou wilt ask Me to make known to thee thereby, that will I do for thee. . . . Do not treat this thing lightly, nor pray for that which is unfitting. Pray that thou mayest know God's secrets and that thou mayest thus receive knowledge about them, and translate all these holy and ancient records that have been hidden, and according to thy faith it shall be given thee. . . . Behold, it is I who have spoken this, and I am the same one as talked to thee from the beginning. . . . Amen! (*The Book of the Covenant*, section 34)

This revelation was written down from Joseph Smith's god, "who never veers to the right or to the left, and does not walk in crooked paths." Oliver Cowdry could therefore safely rejoice in hope of his future wisdom, but when it came down to brass tacks, he could nevertheless not do the translation himself. The "Urim" and "Thumim," "God's gift," and so on, could achieve nothing [p. 66] in the translation of Smith's "Reformed Egyptian," notwithstanding the oaths and promises of the Lord.

Cowdry began to sense a serious doubt rising in his heart, and the situation again became critical for Smith. His dreams of the future and his speculations were close to disintegration. But then help came as usual in the form of a revelation from the Lord to Oliver Cowdry with the following remarkable contents, dated April 1829:

Behold, I say unto thee, My son, that because thou didst not translate—according to that which thou desiredst of Me—and hast begun once more to write down for My servant Joseph Smith, Jr., thus it is My will that thou mayest continue until thou hast completed these records which I have entrusted to him. And behold, I have other records for which I will give thee power to assist in translating. Be patient, My son, for that is wisdom for Me, and it is not necessary for thee to do the translating for the present time. Behold the labor which thou art called to do is that thou write down for My servant Joseph. And behold, it is because thou didst not continue as thou hadst begun after beginning with the translation, that I have removed this gift from thee. Do not complain, My son, forasmuch as it is wisdom with

---

a. By this is meant the Urim and Thummim, presumably.

Me that I have dealt thus with thee. Behold, thou hast not understood; thou believedst that I would give it to thee when thou hadst not considered further than making a request of Me. But behold, I say unto thee, Thou must study it out in thy mind, and then thou mayest ask me whether it is right [to grant it]*; and if it is right, I will cause thy heart to burn within thee; thereby shalt thou know that it is right. But if it is not right, then shalt thou have no such sensation, but thy thoughts shall be so dark that thou wilt forget that which is not right. For this reason thou canst not write down what is holy unless it is given thee from Me. But if thou hadst known this, thou couldst have translated; yet it is not necesary that thou translate at the present time. Behold, it was necessary that thou shouldest make a beginning. But thou wast afraid, and the time is past, and it is not required now. For dost thou not see that I have given My servant Joseph sufficient power to make up for it, and no one of you [p. 67] do I consider to blame!" (*Book of the Covenant*, section 35)

*These words added for clarity.—Trans.

To ascribe to an omniscient and unchangeable God the origination of such a revelation is of course downright blasphemy. One day the Lord finds it necessary to engage Oliver Cowdry to help His servant Joseph to translate, and entrusts "gifts" and "powers" to him which "no might will be able to remove from his hands"; but the next day He reconsiders and tells him that his help is not needed. One day the Lord says, "Verily, verily, as surely as I live, so surely shalt thou receive knowledge of that which thou dost ask for in faith, etc." The next day He asks "His son, Oliver" to "be patient and not to complain" because He is taking back His word and oath, because "it is wisdom with me to deal thus with thee!" says the Lord. What would likely be said about a frail human who acted that way? And yet this is supposed to have come from an omniscient God!

Oliver had done everything the Lord had commanded him in order for him to receive "knowledge"; he had fulfilled his part of the contract, and the Lord finds no fault with him or with Joseph: "None of you do I consider to blame." But what stood in the way of "My son, Oliver"? Why, it was simply this: "He had not understood!" He had been naive enough to believe in Smith's "gold plates in Reformed Egyptian," which were to be translated "by the gift and power of God," but it was by no means in that way that the thing was to be taken. Nor could dictionaries or linguistics be of any help, for no one had ever before heard tell of "Reformed Egyptian." To the general understanding such difficulties would seem to be insuperable. How amazed and light of heart might not Oliver have remained, therefore, when the Lord came and told him, "Behold, thou hast not understood. . . . Behold, I say unto thee, thou must study it out in thy mind!"—Here is the whole mystery of Joseph Smith and Mormonism! Here is the divine origin and appearance of the Book of Mormon! What a simple and natural way to "think it out" or figure a thing out in one's mind, isn't it? The holy scribes had to follow the inspiration of the Holy Spirit as they wrote, but Joseph Smith [p. 68] only had to study it out in his own mind like all other composers of fairy tales and novels.

If we have demonstrated here that Joseph Smith was a deceiver in this matter and the Book of Mormon is a fraud, then every other observation concerning the rise of Mormonism would be superfluous. But for the sake of completeness we shall add a few more detailed items of information about the character of Smith and of the men who came forward as his first witnesses, along with the true origin of the Book of Mormon.

Smith's youthfulness and ignorance are by themselves poor arguments to cite against him, for among the great chosen men of history such persons are often found, and God is certainly almighty enough to carry out His purposes even with those who are lowly and undistinguished among men. On the other hand it is unlikely that God would especially choose an immoral and mendacious person as His instrument for the salvation of men. Many honestly verified testimonies have been contributed by his neighbors and personal acquaintances; some of them we cite at this point[2]:

> We the undersigned are personally acquainted with Joseph Smith Senior's family—with whom the so-called "Golden Bible" had its origin—and we can testify that the male members of the family were not only lazy and indolent, but they

2. A series of sworn affidavits made by acquaintances of Smith's can be found in E. D. Howe's *Mormonism Unveiled* (Painesville, Ohio: E. D. Howe, 1834).

fall into drink, and their word is not to be trusted. We are very glad to be rid of their fellowship.

> Manchester, Ontario County, N.Y.
> November 3, 1833
> (here follow eleven signatures)

We the undersigned have known the Smith family for several years while they were living in the vicinity of this place, and we can testify that we regard them as lacking in such a moral character as could make them deserving of trust in any society whatever. In particular they are notorious for their projects of "revelation," and [p. 69] they spend a good deal of time digging for treasure which they claim is hidden in the earth. The older Smith and his son Joseph in particular are regarded as lacking in moral character and inclined to crime.

> December 4, 1873
> (This was signed by 71 highly respected citizens)

A certain Willard Chase testifies:

> From the time that I became acquainted with Joseph Smith, Jr., I regarded him as a man whose word could hardly be trusted. Since the family became Mormon, their conduct has been even more dishonorable than before. Even though they left this part of the country without paying their debts, yet their creditors nevertheless preferred that to detaining them back here.

Henry Harris gave his oath that "Joseph Smith's truth and veracity were such that he would not believe him under oath. . . . I was once in court on a jury that rejected his testimony because they could not accept it as true."

Levi Lewis says, "I know that Joseph Smith is a liar. Three times I saw him drunk when he was engaged in translating the Book of Mormon. I have heard him say that fornication was not a crime."

Barton Stafford testified before Judge Baldwin: "Joseph Smith Senior was notorious for his drunkenness and the majority of the family followed his example; Joseph Smith, Jr. the prophet, was much addicted. I once saw him drunk in my father's field and in this condition he was talking about his religion."

Not less than 70 sworn testimonies about the Smith family's immoral character express themselves along the same lines. Whatever weight one wants to assign to them, yet it is a settled fact that they have never been refuted. Smith left the area with his family under the pretext of persecution, and so on, on account of his faith. Joseph Smith himself admits to the contrary in his autobiography that he "fell into many serious errors and displayed the weaknesses and corruptions [p. 70] of youth"[3] and so on. In regard to Smith's contradictory accounts relative to the golden plates, we should like to adduce an individual testimony as well.

Peter Ingersoll, one of Smith's most intimate friends, says: "Smith told me that the whole story was a fictional adventure (a hoax), that he had no such book and he didn't think either that it existed. 'But,' said he, 'as I have got the . . . fools fixed, I shall go on with the play.'"

Willard Chase testifies, ". . . Smith came to me to get a chest made to lay his golden Bible in, and he promised me a portion of the book by way of payment. He said it was not permitted him to show it to anyone before two years' time."

Isaac Hale, Smith's father-in-law, relates: "I asked Smith about who would first be permitted to see the book of plates, and he answered that it would be a little child."[4]

"Smith told me," says Rev. N. Lewis, "that it had been commanded him to show the plates to the whole world. At a definite time, about 18 months thereafter, I too would get to see them, but when that time arrived, he said that he had been misled [about that]."*

"Smith told me," says Henry Harris, "that he could not take up the plates until he got married, and that no one with the exception of himself and his wife might see them."

Levi Lewis testifies: "Smith told me that God had fooled him, and that was the reason he had not shown the plates!"

Sophie Lewis relates: "I heard Smith say that the plates could not be opened by any other persons except by his own firstborn, who was going to be a boy." Sophie Lewis happened to be on hand at this birth, and she says that "the child was stillborn and very deformed."

All these sworn testimonies were given by honest and

*These words added for clarity.—Trans.

---

3. For a quotation of this, see *Times and Seasons*, 3:749.
4. An interview with Isaac Hale is found in the *Susquehanna Register*, May 1, 1834, Susquehanna, Pennsylvania.

disinterested persons, so far as one can tell. The prophet could not controvert them, and he left [p. 71] his part of the country where he could expect to find neither proselytes nor any credence. But before proving the truth about his crooked and self-contradictory "revelations," he procured for himself testimony from eleven people who are found in print in every edition of the Book of Mormon. These we must now take under consideration.

In March 1829 Smith received a revelation (cf. *The Book of the Covenant*, section 32) in which the Lord says to Martin Harris, "I will give power to these three witnesses that they may see and behold these things (the plates, the Urim and Thummim, etc.) as they are; and to no one else will I give this power to receive this same witness in this generation!" In the month of June he receives another revelation (*The Book of the Covenant*, section 40) given to Oliver Cowdry, David Whitmer, Martin Harris, who are the three chosen witnesses, in which it is said:

> Behold, I say unto you that ye must rely upon My word, and if ye do so with all your heart, ye will get to see the tablets, and also the breastplate, Laban's sword and the Urim and Thummim. . . . And ye shall all testify that ye have seen them just as My servant Joseph has seen them. . . . Therefore ye have received the same power, the same gift and the same faith as he . . .

This remarkable testimony in its entirety goes as follows:

> Let it be known before all nations, races, languages and people to whom this work shall come, that by means of the grace of God the Father and of our Lord Jesus Christ we have seen the plates which contain this record, which is a record about the people of Nephi and also about their brothers the Lamanites, along with the people of Jared, who came from the Tower (Babel), concerning whom it has been spoken. We know also that they have been translated by means of the grace and power of God, for His voice has revealed that to us. Therefore it is with certainty that we know that the work is truth. We testify also that we have seen the engraved symbols which are upon the plates and that by the power of God, not by the power of man, they have been shown to us. We declare in carefully chosen words that an angel of God came down from heaven and brought the plates and laid

them down [p. 72] before our eyes so that we saw the plates and the words engraved upon them. We know that it is by the grace of God and the Father and of our Lord Jesus Christ that we saw them and we bear witness that these things are true, and that it is wondrous in our eyes. Nevertheless the voice of the Lord commanded us to bear testimony about them, and in order to be obedient to God's command we do bear witness about these things and we know that if we are steadfast in Christ, then shall our garments be free of the blood of all men, and we shall be found spotless before the judgment seat of Christ and shall live with him forever in heaven. And glory be to the Father, the Son and to the Holy Spirit, who are one God, Amen! Oliver Cowdry, David Whittmer, Martin Harris.

In the two revelations of March 1829 which were quoted previously the Lord says that these three witnesses are to see the breastplate (of the high priest), Laban's sword, the Urim and the Thummin, along with the plates of gold. They receive a command at that time to "bear witness" about them, and yet we do not find a single word about these things in the cited testimony. "Ye shall all witness that ye have seen them, just as My servant Joseph has seen them" was the way it was put. But since they do not testify about these things, it is reasonable to infer that they did not see them, either. Furthermore: ". . . Ye have seen them, just as My servant Joseph has seen them"—consequently Joseph Smith didn't see them either! There are also some incomprehensible expressions that are used in the testimony: An angel came down from heaven to show them the plates before their very eyes and "this appeared wonderful in their eyes"; but just the same, the angel of the Lord commanded them to bear witness of them. "And it is in order to be obedient to the Lord's command that we bear witness of these things." If these three witnesses to the truth (?)* had seen what they claimed they had, they would undoubtedly have willingly told it forth everywhere* as a great miracle; but rather it was only that they might be "obedient" and "follow after the Lord's command" that they related it—or more accurately said, they sign their names to a testimony composed by Joseph Smith.

There is another strange circumstance in connection with the revelation to Martin Harris in the year 1829. That

*The question mark appears in the original edition, added for irony.
—Trans.

*Literally, "to high and low."
—Trans.

is, the Lord [p. 73] at that time declared: "I will give to these three witnesses power to see these things, and to no one else will I give this power to receive this testimony in this generation." And yet Joseph Smith wants to require the people believe the following testimony which he gave a year later, in 1830, and which is found quoted in the Book of Mormon:

The Testimony of Eight Men

Let it be know to all nations, races, tongues and peoples to whom this work may come, that Joseph Smith Junior, the translator of this work has shown us the plates which are here spoken of and which had the appearance of gold. Moreover we have held in our hands many of the pages which the aforesaid Smith has translated, and likewise we have seen the engraved symbols on them, which appear to be like ancient work of a peculiar sort. And we bear witness of this in well-considered words that the aforesaid Smith has shown us; for we have seen and felt and know with certainty that the aforesaid Smith has the plates of which we have spoken. And we give forth our names to the world concerning that which we have seen, and we lie not. May God be our witness thereto.

Christin Whittmer, Jacob Whittmer, Peter Whittmer Junior, John Whittmer, Hiram Page, Joseph Smith Senior, Hyrum Smith, Samuel Smith.[b]

This testimony stands in direct contradiction to the revelation of the Lord in March 1829, which declares that *only three* witnesses are to see and witness about these things during this generation. Perhaps it was for this reason that Smith himself arrogated to himself the authority to show the plates to the eight men that an angel had to descend from heaven in order that the three might be witnesses. They saw and testified only by means of "faith" and "the commandment of the Lord." The eight see and feel and bear witness *contrary to* the Lord's commandment. From a judicial standpoint both of these testimonials are completely meaningless, because they are [p. 74] confirmed by oath before no lawful court whatever, and they

---

b. Therefore there were four Whittmers, one Page who was related to Oliver Cowdry, and three Smiths—the prophet's father and his two brothers. The trustworthiness of the testimony is significantly impaired by the fact that the witnesses were so closely related to each other as individuals.

are found to lack either a date or a location of their occurrence. The style in both documents shows that Joseph Smith composed them himself, and their mutual contradiction clearly enough betrays them to be a wretched deception. Even apart from that not even the character of the witnesses themselves affords any special guarantee for the trustworthiness of their testimonies. In a revelation which Smith had occasion to impart to Harris in 1830, it is stated among other things: "And again I command thee to give generously of thy possessions to the printing of the Book of Mormon. And pay the debt thou hast entered into with the printers (*Book of the Covenant*, section 84). . . . And again I command thee, Thou shalt not covet thy neighbor's wife or seek for thy neighbor's life." In 1837 the prophet remarks in his organ *The Elder's Journal* regarding Martin Harris:

> There are niggers with a white skin as well as those of a black skin—Grandmother Parish, and others who serve as lackeys, such as Martin Harris! But they are so far beneath my contempt that it would be too great a sacrifice for a gentleman to take notice of them.

That must have been hard on poor Harris, since Smith at that time had completely ruined him.[5] It was not much better for Oliver Cowdry and David Whittmer.[6] On April 6, 1838, both of them were expelled from the Mormon Church, and in the accusation raised against them by Sidney Rigdon, they are blamed for "standing in the vanguard of a gang of deceivers, thieves, liars and bandits of the blackest stripe in order to deceive and rob from the saints." In the church organ *Times and Seasons* Joseph Smith says that these two were "diligent in arousing strife and commotion among the brethren in Missouri in 1830," and he asks, "Is not their conscience like one that has been branded with a hot iron—are they not murderers in their heart?" Sidney Rigdon's accusation presented to the Conference in Independence, Missouri, was likewise stated:

---

5. Twice in the *Doctrine and Covenants* Harris is called a "wicked man" (see 3:12-13; 10:6-7).
6. In a letter dated December 16, 1838, Joseph Smith made the following statement: "David Whitmer, Oliver Cowdery, and Martin Harris are too mean to mention and we had liked to have forgotten them" (cited in the *Documentary History of the Church*, 3:232).

"They sought to destroy Joseph Smith's reputation by falsely insinuating that he had practiced immorality." Hyrum Smith, Joseph's brother, finally blamed Oliver Cowdry for going into his (Hyrum's) house while he was in prison, and "removing [p. 75] a number of objects and compelling my aged father by threatening him with mob attack to give him a deed for one hundred acres of land as payment for a promissory note of $160 that he claimed I had contracted, but which was a mere falsehood."

As for the other eight witnesses, well, we should only observe that they have long ago abandoned Mormonism. Smith's fellow witnesses, or as they may also be termed, his fellow culprits, thus became (remarkably enough) the first ones who showed by word and deed that they had neither faith in nor conviction concerning the things which they themselves had confirmed; they were the first to repudiate their own testimony.[7]

With the aid of these facts, which are open information to everyone who seeks them, the reader is hopefully in a position to judge whether the Book of Mormon is "of divine origin" or not. We would only repeat Orson Pratt's dictum: "The Book of Mormon is of such a character that if it be true, no one can be saved who rejects it; and if it be false, then no one can be saved who accepts it!"

From what source does the Book of Mormon have its real origin? Joseph Smith was at that time too young and too ignorant to be its original author.[8] One is almost compelled to believe that he was really in possession of certain plates and other materials which furnished the basis for its appearance, and likewise for the many stories which he understood how to make the witnesses believe. It is probable that the transcript which Joseph Smith gave to Martin Harris and which he brought to Professor Anton in New York in 1830 must have been copied by Smith from some engraved tables. But by no means does this prove that Smith received these plates in the manner he stated, and far less that he translated them by means of "the gift and power of God," or by a pair of gem-spectacles which he called "Urim and Thummim." Martin Harris states that

---

7. For a study of the character of the witnesses, see *Mormonism: Shadow or Reality?* pp. 50-59.
8. Actually, Smith was in his early twenties during the time the *Book of Mormon* was written.

at first the learned professor recognized Smith's transcript as genuine and declared that the written symbols were Egyptian, Chaldee, and Assyrian, and he gave him a written certification thereto. [p. 76] But as soon as he heard the story of the appearance of the plates, he took the certification back and tore it to pieces.

The Mormons very cleverly capitalized on this interview between Harris and the professors by maintaining that this was the fulfillment of a prophecy in Isaiah 29:11. Therefore a few years later Professor Anton published a declaration in this regard: "The written signs were arranged in vertical rows somewhat like the Chinese style and they made up the most peculiar mixture I have ever seen. They were Greek, Hebrew, and all kinds of letters which either deliberately or out of ignorance were more or less misshapen, mixed up with various imitations of half-moons, stars, and other objects of nature. Then the whole thing ended with a plain imitation of the Mexican zodiac."

Professor Rafinesque in the *Atlantic Journal*, 1832, describes some hieroglyphs from Otulum in Mexico which were likewise written "from the top to the bottom like Chinese." This is at least a suggestion that Joseph Smith is not the only one in the State of New York who has found engraved plates from olden times, as the following document indicates:

On April 16, 1843 a respectable merchant named Robert Witley began digging in a hill near the city. When he had reached a depth of ten feet he came upon a stone. On the twenty-fourth he came out to the hill together with some other citizens, and after they had made an adequate opening we found a group of stones that appeared to have been burned with an intense heat. When a full two feet of such stones had been removed, we found ashes and charcoal and also some human bones, which likewise appeared to have been burned. Near this spot (the Eciphalen) was found a set of six brass plates resembling a church bell, smaller at the top and at the bottom, and they had a hole with a ring in the smaller end that held the plates together. The ring and the clamps resembled iron and were greatly rusted. At first glance the plates looked like copper and appeared to be filled with letters. The group agreed [p. 77] that I should clean the plates and consequently I took them home with me and washed them with a woolen rag in soapy water. But when this proved inadequate, I used a solution of sulphuric acid, which got them completely clean. Then it appeared that they were indeed inscribed with signs which no one has up until now been able to read. They were found about twelve feet down in the hill by me and the citizens of Kinderhook.

W. P. Harris, M.D.

At the same time the following documents were published:

We, the undersigned, citizens of Kinderhook declare, that while we were engaged in excavating a large hill in our vicinity Mr. R. Whitley found six bell-shaped brass plates which were covered with some sort of ancient writing. The plates were heavily corroded with rust, and the ring and clamps crumbled in pieces when they were touched.

Robert Whiley		George Dickenson
W. Langnecker	G. W. Ward	J. R. Sharp
Ira G. Curtis		Janette Grubb
W. Hanes		W. Fugate[9]

The hieroglyphs on these plates resembled those which Professor Anton and Rafinesque talked about and were written like Chinese in columns from top to bottom. The only difference is that Wiley [sic] found his while he was digging for water, and Joseph Smith found his while he was digging for treasure which was supposed to have been buried by the notorious buccaneer Captain Kidd in the western part of New York State.

---

9. The names should be as follows: Robert Whiley, W. Longnecker, G. W. F. Ward, Ira S. Curtis, George Deckenson, J. R. Sharp, Fayette Grubb, W. P. Harris, and W. Fugate.

Actually, these "Kinderhook Plates" dug up by Whiley turned out to be forgeries that fooled Joseph Smith. In a statement dated June 30, 1879, W. Fugate, a friend of Whiley's, admitted that they had made the plates in their shop and buried them the night before their discovery. Joseph Smith, not knowing that they were fabrications, examined the plates and claimed that they contained the history of an ancient Egyptian (see *Documentary History of the Church*, 5:372-79). One of the plates is still is in existence today at the Chicago Historical Society and was recently scientifically analyzed. Mormon scholar Stanley Kimball announced the scientific results in the *Ensign* (vol. 11, no. 8, pp. 66ff), where he admits that they were a product of the nineteenth century and were not authentic ancient plates. Ahmanson would not have known of the forgeries as Fugate did not go public until 1879.

In regard to the origin of the "Urim and Thummim," when Willard Chase gave a sworn statement to Judge King in Wayne County, New York, it was to the following effect: "In 1822 he and Joseph Smith (who was then seventeen) were digging a well, and then he found a peculiar stone about twenty feet down from the surface. Joseph Smith put it in his hat and claimed that he could see into the stone when he held the hat over his face." [p. 78] On the following day Smith borrowed the stone, which Chase was rather unwilling to give him, and shortly after that Smith began to tell about many marvelous things he could see in the stone. Chase demanded the stone back from him. In 1825 Smith again borrowed the stone under the pretext that he wanted it for a very important reason and he promised to return it soon. In the following year, 1826, Chase sent a messenger for the stone, but Smith refused to deliver it back to him.—"Smith told me that he found his golden Bible and said, 'if it had not been for your stone I could not have received the book.' He then asked me to make him a box to put the books in, but this I refused to do." In 1830 Chase again demanded the stone back from Hiram Smith, the prophet's brother, in the presence of Martin Harris. "Hiram said that he could not have it, because Joseph was using it to translate his new Bible with. When I said that it was my stone and that I had to have it, Martin Harris became furious, called me a liar and grabbed me by the collar. Hiram also took part in the fight, showed me his clenched fists and treated me in a shameful way." Chase never did get his stone back.

This testimony is confirmed by a sworn statement that Isaac Hale, Smith's father-in-law, furnished:

> I became acquainted with Joseph Smith for the first time in November 1825. He was in the service of some men who were called treasure-hunters and it was his assignment to see—or to pretend that he could see—(the location of) minerals or hidden treasure with the help of a stone which he put in this hat and held in front of his face. In the same fashion he claimed that he could read and translate the plates with the stone in his hat and the hat over his face, while the plates were hidden underneath.

Isaac Hale's testimony has special importance because a portion of the "translation" took place in his home, until

Hale became weary of the deception and showed the translator the door.[10]

In all likelihood, therefore, Joseph would have been in possession of certain natural objects that would have served [p. 79] him as a sort of camouflage during the carrying out of a deception. And as for his witnesses, the crudest bandit can as a rule quite easily secure some fellow thieves; why should not a man gifted in so many lines as Joseph Smith be capable of obtaining henchmen and accomplices?

It is obvious from the contents of the Book of Mormon that at the time he began it, Joseph Smith had not the slightest idea of its becoming the basis for a new doctrine or the foundation for a new religion, for it does not contain a single new principle or new revelation within the orbit of Christian dogma.[11] The Book of Mormon, so far as its contents are concerned, consists of historical and religious narrations.

Its historical portion comprises a period of time beginning shortly after the destruction of "the tower of Babel," and it ends about A.D. 500. The work as a whole sets forth in some detail the population and earliest history of America. Jared and his family were the first who emigrated to America shortly after the "confusion of Babel;" but his descendants were completely annihilated by the race of Lehi, which arrived from Jerusalem about 600 B.C.—All the righteous of the Lehites, who belonged to the tribe of Manasseh, came to an end around A.D. 400, whereas the ungodly race lives on still, that is, the present American Indians. At lastly there were some Jews, the so-called people of Zarahemla, who eleven years after Lehi's family, emigrated from Jerusalem to America. But the majority of them died out through warfare, and the remainder united with the descendants of Lehi. The history of these various nations' wars and migrations, etc., was always written down by their prophets on gold or brass plates, which they preserved and handed down from generation to generation. Three hundred eighty-four years after Christ these plates

10. Isaac Hale's testimony first appeared in the *Susquehanna Register*, May 1, 1834.
11. The *Book of Mormon* neither contains any of the distinctive doctrines of the Mormon church. There is no mention of three degrees of heaven, baptism for the dead, eternal marriage, God being a man, men becoming gods, etc.

fell into the hands of one of Levi's descendants named Mormon, who in turn handed on a copy of the entire collection to his son, Moroni. Moroni added to this the history of "Jared's people" and placed all of the plates into a chest, which he buried in a hill in the State [p. 80] of New York in A.D. 400. In this chest, then, the plates were supposed to have lain, until they were given over to Joseph Smith on September 22, 1827.

All of the religious content of the Book of Mormon was derived from the Bible. In it is found not only the same doctrines (in part, at least) as in the Bible,[12] but also the words, and identical sentences, yes even entire chapters— like 6 of the prophet Isaiah, for example, and a chapter from Malachi, three from the gospel of Matthew, and a chapter from Paul's First Epistle to the Corinthians.[13] In his excellent "History of Mormonism" John Hyde says:

> From page 2 to 428 which purports to deal with events which took place 600 years before the birth of Christ, I have counted no less than 298 quotations from the New Testament consisting of paragraphs or sentences. These Biblical quotations are found inserted here and there throughout the historical portion of the Book of Mormon, and it quotes them word for word and it fully resembles the original in the English Bible. But despite this the Mormons have at all times busied themselves with attacking the Bible as altogether untrustworthy on account of the many mistakes which it has suffered from being in the hands of uninspired and dishonest translators.

Thus the Book of Mormon does not have the slightest significance in religious understanding, and in regard to esthetics it is found to be so full of self-contradictions and absurdities, like some wretched defective who would like to downgrade every other author except an ignorant boy like Joseph Smith. It is downright ridiculous to accept an

---

12. Examples of doctrines found in the *Book of Mormon* that are similar or the same as biblical teachings are: God is a spirit (Alma 18:24-28; 22:9-11; 31:15); the Trinity (2 Nephi 31:21; Alma 11:44); God is unchanging (Moroni 8:18; Mormon 9:9, 19); only one God (Alma 11:26-31; 12:44).

13. For an excellent study of the use of the Bible in the *Book of Mormon* see H. Michael Marquardt, *The Use of the Bible in the Book of Mormon and Early Nineteenth Century Events reflected in the Book of Mormon* (Salt Lake City: Utah Lighthouse Ministry).

all-wise God as the source of such a botched piece of work.

The original motive for Joseph Smith's account of the golden plates and the Book of Mormon becomes evident from the following testimony which was furnished by Abigail Harris, the sister of Martin Harris on November 28, 1833:

> I was visiting Martin Harris at the beginning of the winter of 1828 and at the same time I came into fellowship with Joseph Smith, Senior and his wife. The affair relating to the so-called golden Bible furnished a chief subject for conversation. I gave special heed to this because I wanted to know the whole truth concerning the matters being discussed. They told me that the rumor [p. 81] about Joseph Smith's discovery of the golden plates was true, and that he was now in Harmony, Pennsylvania in order to translate them. The old lady stated further that when the book had been translated, the plates would be shown to the public. The entry fee would be set at 25 cents. She figured that this would bring in a huge sum of money each year, and that the book could be sold at a high price, since it was something completely new. They had received orders to borrow as much money as possible in order to defray their present expenses, and later to pay this loan back in gold. Whatever remained over should be kept for the benefit of the family and the children. The old lady took me into another room and after closing the door she said: "Can you lend me four or five dollars until we are done with this affair? The Spirit says that you will receive it back fourfold!" I answered that when I gave, I expected nothing in return, and in regard to money, I had none to lend. Two months later Martin Harris and his wife Lucy were in the house. During our conversation concerning the Mormons Madame Harris expressed the wish that her husband might abandon them, for she regarded the whole thing as a fraud. I heard Mr. Harris answer this by saying: "Let it be that it is a deception, if you will just leave me in peace, I will make some money from it!"—I both heard and saw what I have shared and it is still alive in my recollection. I am telling the truth and not lying, as God is my witness.

Therefore there was a factor of financial speculation on the side of both Joseph Smith and Martin Harris. Martin's own wife, Lucy, furnished the following testimony:

I leave it to the world to judge whether the religion of the Mormons is true or false, but its influence upon Martin Harris has been such that he has become more quick-tempered and spiteful toward me. His entire purpose was to make money by it. One day when we were visiting Peter Harris (Abigail Harris' husband) I asked him to give up his involvement with the Smith family, since their religion was completely false. To this he answered [p. 82] ". . . if you will just leave me in peace I will make some money out of it! . . ." It is futile for the Mormons to deny these facts, for they are well known to his former neighbors.

That the prophet's parents were not unaware or disinterested in the financial speculation is shown by the following testimony of a certain Joseph Capron: ". . . Joseph Smith, Jr. maintained to the very last that he had found his plates. He believed this enterprise would help the family out of its financial embarrassment. His father told me that when the book was printed, from the profit that its sale would bring in they would be able to make a lucky strike in treasure hunting. From our conversation at that time I had no idea that the contents of the book were of a religious nature or that it had any connection with revelations. He called it a speculation and said: "When it is finished, my family will assume a higher position than most people in society."

As we have indicated, the religious part of the Book of Mormon is taken word for word out of the Bible; in order to eliminate the slightest thought of revelation we are fortunately in a position to point out where its historical contents came from.

John Spaulding, a brother of Solomon Spaulding of Crawford, Pennsylvania, furnishes the following testimony:

Solomon Spaulding was born in Ashford, Connecticut in 1751. In his younger years he had a fondness for literary studies. After leaving school he studied at Plainfield Academy and there he manifested such great competence that he surpassed most of his classmates. Later on he pursued studies in this field at Dartmouth College for the purpose of taking an examination for the pastorate; there he received an A.M. degree and was ordained. After three or four years of pastoral work he moved to Cherry Valley, New York, and began a mercantile business in company with his brother Josiah. When I visited him three years later I found that his business had failed and that he had a considerable indebtedness. He told me that he had written a book which he had in mind to get printed so that with the money [p. 83] he would receive from its sale he would pay back a portion of his debt. He read several portions of the book to me, the title of which was "The Discovered Manuscript." It was a historical novel about America's earliest inhabitants, in which he adduced evidence that America's Indians were descended from the Jews, or were the lost tribes of Israel. It gave a precise description of their journey from Jerusalem by land and by sea, until they arrived in America under the leadership of *Nephi* and *Lehi*. Later on they had a division and a quarrel, and they separated into two nations. One of them was called "Nephites" and the other "Lamanites." Cruel and bloody wars ensued with a great loss of life on both sides. They buried their dead in some good-sized hills, and this is the reason for the many Indian mounds in this country. Their arts and sciences were also intensified in order to show forth by them the origin of the many remarkable antiquities which are found in North and South America. I have recently read the Book of Mormon and I was much surprised to see in it almost the same historical narrative, including even the same names, and so on, as occurred in my brother's manuscript. I very well remember that he wrote in the ancient style and began almost every sentence with, "And it came to pass . . ." or "Now it came to pass," just as is the case in the Book of Mormon. According to my belief and conviction the Book of Mormon is the same as that which my brother wrote, with the exception of its religious content. But I cannot say in what way it came into the hands of Joseph Smith.

Martha Spaulding, the wife of John Spaulding, testifies:

I knew Solomon Spaulding personally for twenty years and was in his home before he left Connecticut. At that time he was about to write a historical novel about America's first inhabitants, who would be depicted as an enlightened and warlike people. For several years he had claimed that America's original inhabitants were descendants from some of the lost tribes of Israel and he set forth this idea in the book aforementioned. The long amount of time which has elapsed since I read the book is such that I can only remember a few of the most important episodes in [p. 84] his manuscript; but the names "Nephi" and "Lehi" still live on in my recollection, for they were the leading heroes in his narrative. They were the commanders of an organization (of people) who first came from Jerusalem. He gave a detailed description of their journey from Jerusalem both by land and by sea until they reached America. Then the quarrels arose between their governors and this brought about their settlement in different regions. One group was called the "Lamanites" and the other the "Nephites." There arose a terrible war between them which often covered the earth with the slain. And the fact that they buried their dead in good-sized hills is the origin of the many Indian mounds in this country. I have read the Book of Mormon and this has brought vividly back Solomon Spaulding's composition to my remembrance. I don't have the slightest doubt that the historical portion of the book is the same as that which I read and heard read to me over twenty years ago. The old-fashioned style and the expressions, "And it came to pass, etc." are the same!

Henry Lake, an erstwhile companion of Solomon Spaulding, gave testimony along the same line in September 1833, as follows: "I left New York State in 1820," he says,

and I came to this place, (Conneaut in Ashtabula County, Ohio) on the following January 1st. Soon after my arrival I went into partnership with Solomon Spaulding for the purpose of completing a foundry which he had begun one or two years previously. He very often read aloud to me portions of a manuscript that he was in the process of writing. He called it "The Discovered Manuscript" and he represented it as having been found in Conneaut. I spent many hours listening to his compositions and became very familiar with their contents. He wanted me to help him get his production into print, and he assumed that a work of this sort would get into speedy circulation. It was my intention to assist him, but since the foundry did not live up to our expectations, our business went to pieces, and after that I didn't want to concern myself with the publication of the book. In this book the American Indians were presented as descending from [p. 85] the tribes of Israel. It gave a description of their journey from Jerusalem, along with their numerous large-scale wars. One time when he read to me that tragic account about "Laban," I called his attention to something in it that appeared inconsistent to me. He thought that he had rectified the blunders, but when I read the Book of Mormon I was surprised to find that they were still there just as he had read them to me at that time. Some months later I borrowed the so-called Golden Bible, the Book of Mormon, and stuck it in my pocket. I took it home and thought no more about it. But after a week had gone by my wife found the book in my coat pocket and began to read aloud from it while I was lying on the bed. She had not read twenty minutes before I became surprised at hearing the same narratives in it that Spaulding had read to me twenty years before from "The Discovered Manuscript." After that I examined the Golden Bible more carefully, and I feel not the slightest hesitation in saying that the historical portion primarily—if not in its entirety—is taken from "The Discovered Manuscript." I remember well that I called Spaulding's attention to his frequent use of, "And it came to pass. . . !" or, "Now it happened that. . . !" to a ridiculous extreme.— Spaulding left the place in 1812, and I gave him the money to travel to Pittsburgh, where he said he would get the book printed and would pay me. But since then I never heard from him or his writing until I saw it in "The Book of Mormon."

The three witnesses quoted from, along with several (others) in agreement with him, who knew Spaulding but did not know Joseph Smith, explain the origin of the Book of Mormon clearly enough. Now it is only a matter of showing how Joseph Smith came into possession of Spaulding's manuscript. Spaulding wrote it during the years 1810-12 in Ohio. In 1812 he moved to Pittsburgh, lived there two years, and then went to Amity, Pennsylvania, where he died in 1816. After his death his widow moved to Onondago County, New York, lived there until 1818, and then made her home in Hartwick, Oswego County, in the same state, until 1832. She expresses it as her conviction that that manuscript, [p. 86] along with several others, was put in a trunk and lay there during her sojourn in Hartwick from 1820 to 1830. According to his own account Joseph Smith was in the service of a man named Stowell, who was a neighbor of the folks in the house where the trunk was kept. After the Book of Mormon was published and became well known, the aforementioned trunk was opened and investigated, but it then contained only one manuscript; the rest of the papers were gone. The manuscript still remaining was the beginning of a novel that represented the Indians as descending from the Latin race. Spaulding had given up this plan after writing only a few pages, and he began another manuscript which never came to light later on. Mrs. Spaulding declares that the trunk was filled with her husband's manuscripts, among which was the one under discussion. Who was it that laid hands on them? The deduction is at least plausible indeed that Joseph Smith was the man. From 1825 to 1827 Smith relates that he "received instruction." That took him not quite as long a period of time to adapt "The Discovered Manuscript" as it took Spaulding to write it! With the Bible and Spaulding's manuscript in front of him, it was no longer any miracle for even a Joseph Smith to put together a work like the Book of Mormon, especially when he had two such scribes as Martin Harris and Oliver Cowdry for his secretaries! Within two years a young man like Joseph Smith can, if he wishes, learn and achieve many things. From the American pulpit there sounds out not only God's Word and the gospel according to the interpretations of numerous sects, but also the burning questions of the day come in for discussion.[14]

Therefore it was quite easy for the young prophet, even without the aid of miracles or book-learning, to gain possession of the religious, poetic, philosophic phrases and sentences which are found inserted into the Book of Mormon, in the midst of the basic text of Spaulding and the Bible. It is only in the framing of his religious dogmas that Smith manifests an unusual stupidity, in connection with a

---

14. Mr. Ahmanson's view that the *Book of Mormon* was taken from one of Spaulding's books has not been totally accepted by many experts in Mormon history, although there has recently been an interesting work on the subject by Vernal Holley, *Book of Mormon Authorship: A Closer Look* (Ogden, Utah: Zenos Publications, 1983). However, there were other works that Joseph Smith could have used in writing the *Book of Mormon*. Among these was Ethan Smith's *View of the Hebrews*, which was published five to eight years prior to the publishing of the *Book of Mormon*. The parallels between this book and the *Book of Mormon* are so striking that Mormon historian and General Authority B. H. Roberts was forced to admit that *View of the Hebrews* "could well have furnished structural outlines for the Book of Mormon" (*A Book of Mormon Study*, p. 8 in the reprint by the Utah Lighthouse Ministry, Salt Lake City). There is also an excellent review of Roberts's manuscript by Wesley P. Walters entitled "The Origin of the Book of Mormon," *Journal of Pastoral Practice*, vol. 3, no. 3 (Phillipsburg, N. J.: Presbyterian and Reformed).

lack of historical knowledge [p. 87] and discrimination. The following report of the Book of Mormon will show this.

During the reign of King Zedekiah "Lehi" and his family left Jerusalem in order to migrate to America. After Lehi had gone on his way for some distance it occurred to him that he did not have with him any of the Holy Scriptures of his people. Therefore he sent his son Nephi back to Jerusalem to steal these from Laban, one of Lehi's relatives. Nephi carried out his mission with great thoroughness. He killed Laban, broke into his house, and took away not only Laban's writings but also Laban's servants! A bandit could probably have performed a similar deed, but Nephi was modest, and as soon as he arrived back in the wilderness, he thanked the Lord for his help and support in this connection! Laban's brass plates appear, by the way, to contain the Five Books of Moses, "the Jewish history from the beginning until King Zedekiah and the writings of the contemporary prophets." (Cf. the Book of Mormon, pages 7-12.)

The same Nephi begins the Book of Mormon by relating that his father Lehi had "lived all his days in Jerusalem." Concerning himself he informs us that "I am making a record in my father's language, which is the learning of the Jews and the language of the Egyptians!"

The stupidity of such a claim soon appears; one only has to ask, "What basis is there for believing that the Jews recorded their inscriptions on plates of brass?" When did the language of the Egyptians become the scholarship of the Jews? When did the Jews write down the Law of Moses and the Prophets in Egyptian? How could a young Jew who had lived all his life in Jerusalem take to writing Egyptian and call it "my father's language"? Anyone who has any slight knowledge of the Jews of that period—or even of our own time—knows without doubt that the Hebrew language was just as holy to the Jews as the Law itself, which is read to them in that tongue. They both constitute an essential part of their worship. After 1800 years of dispersion and persecution we still find the Law in Jewish synagogues and everywhere else among their true confessors written or printed [p. 88] in Hebrew. In Zedekiah's time, incidentally, the Jews wrote the Law of Moses on parchment, papyrus, or similar material, but by no means on plates of brass.

It is also especially strange that the Law and the other Jewish scriptures should be found in the possession of a Jewish civilian at the time when Lehi left Jerusalem. For shortly before this time they were very hard to get hold of among all the Jewish people. That is to say, in 2 Kings, chapters 22 and 23, it is related how the high priest Hilkiah found the Book of the Law in the house of the Lord, and he exclaimed: "I have found the Book of the Law in the Lord's house!" And when Stephan* brought it to King Josiah, he became so alarmed that he tore his clothes and called together all of the inhabitants of Jerusalem that they might hear the words of the Lord which had been found in the Temple!†

*Here the author has confused the spelling of the name of the king's secretary; it was Shapan, not Stephan. —Trans.

But the history of Christendom in the Book of Mormon far surpasses these circumstances in its colossal absurdity. All that the four gospels relate regarding the conception of the virgin Mary, the birth of Christ, the most noteworthy events in the life of Jesus, His death, His resurrection, and His ascension to heaven, etc., were allegedly known and described in detail among the Nephites in America *four hundred years before the birth of Christ!* These people in America called themselves "Christians" a hundred years before Christ was born and two hundred years before the first Christian congregation in Antioch assumed this label (Acts 11:20).* Also contained in the Book of Mormon are accounts of how Christ after His resurrection visited these extraordinarily favored Nephites in America, and instructed them in the things pertaining to the kingdom of God.

*See footnote†.

*This occurrence in Antioch would have happened around A.D. 60. Thus Ahmanson's figure of 200 years here is off by about half a century. —Ed.

We must repeat again that Smith's first idea with regard to the history about the golden plates and the Book of Mormon was purely a financial speculation. It was in order to carry through his plans with Martin Harris and

---

†Perhaps in fairness to Joseph Smith it might be pointed out that the excitement caused by the discovery of the ancient temple copy of the Pentateuch by no means proves that there were no other more recent copies of it in circulation; the discovery of a first-edition 1611 copy of the King James Version might cause a similar stir among us even in the present day. The mere fact that none of the idol-worshiping nobles or priests could raise any protest against the stern prohibitions of the Mosaic Law is strong evidence that they were already aware of its strictures against idolatrous worship on the "high places," even though they had been totally neglected during the reigns of Manasseh and Amon. Mr. Ahmanson seems to have overlooked these factors in drawing the deduction that there was only one copy of the Pentateuch left in all of Jerusalem. —Trans.

others that he brought in the religious element and according as the plan about forming a new religion began to mature in his mind, he entered upon his role as a prophet.

Neither Joseph Smith's personality nor his mystical Book of Mormon would nevertheless have converted many to this new teaching had it not been for men like Sidney Rigdon, [p. 89] Parley Pratt, and Orson Pratt among others who possessed real knowledge and a respectable character, and contributed new strength and dignity to the faltering system by interpreting many of the prophecies and revelations of Scripture in a clever way and applying them literally in favor of Mormonism.

A book that suffers from so many grievous defects as the Book of Mormon cannot naturally form a secure foundation for a religion of divine origin. Nor does the Bible really belong to the Mormons, who use it only as a decoy for their missionary expeditions. The whole system of Mormonism is built upon the circumstance that its leader, whoever he may be, calls himself a "prophet." The moment Brigham Young or "Bill Hickman" assumes this title and is regarded as a prophet, his power is absolute and his authority unlimited even more unquestionably than kings who rule "by the grace of God."

God is presumed to speak to the prophet, and the latter speaks in turn to the people, who are constantly driven forward by a gang of corrupt bishops, priests, elders, and so on, without having time or opportunity to think over the consequences of their various activities. If one or another of them should venture to feel scruples or doubts, then he is "possessed of Satan" and a damned "apostate," contact with whom every "saint" must fear and avoid. According to Brigham Young's teaching such a person must be delivered over as soon as possible to the "destroying angels" of the Church, that his blood may be poured out as an atoning sacrifice for his errors.

8 The Origin of Mormonism and Its Progress in the United States

[p. 90] Joseph Smith, the founder of Mormonism, was born December 23, 1805, in Sharon, Windsor County, in the State of Vermont. In April 1815 his father, who was also named Joseph Smith, moved from Sharon to Palmyra, Ontario County, in the State of New York, and four years later to the town of Manchester in the same county. Thus it was Manchester that became the point of departure for no less a personality than "the Prophet." Not a prophet like those of the Hebrews, who as they preached the word of the Lord despised the world with its vanities and vices and lived apart in the holes and clifts of the earth—no indeed! But a prophet who, like Mohammed, was called not only to deliver pure doctrine and true faith to the world, but also called to rule and reign over it. In 1820, hence when he was fifteen years old, Joseph Smith received his first revelation, when he was out in a nearby forest in order to pray for enlightenment in regard to which of the many religious parties with which he had come in contact was the true and rightful one. It was just about this time that one of the frequently occurring religious "awakenings" (revivals) was dominant in his area, and nearly all of the local denominations were taking part in it. The Smith family consisted of nine children: three daughters and six sons, of whom Joseph was the youngest. He appeared to feel most attracted to Methodism, but the mother, two of his brothers, and one sister allowed themselves to be converted to Presbyterianism. [p. 91] Under these circumstances frequent discussions and disputes naturally arose quite often concerning the greater or lesser biblical basis of the various sects, and so on, and so it was quite natural that a fifteen-year-old boy who was himself groping for the truth might have become quite confused and disturbed in his mind about this. "While I was occupied with prayer," he related of himself, "I was surrounded with a thick darkness which appeared to threaten me with complete destruction." He then saw a light coming down upon his head, and two personages whose radiance surpassed all description were hovering in that brilliance. One of these persons called Joseph by name and said as he pointed at the other one, "This is My beloved Son, hear thou Him!" Thereupon Joseph came to know that he should not unite with any denomination at all; for they were all "corrupted and abhorrent in the eyes of the Lord" and so on.[1] When he came to himself, he was lying upon his back and looking up toward heaven.[a] That is about the way that Joseph Smith himself recounts his first vision. It is hardly plausible that he made up the entire story out of thin air, and so attempts have been made to give various explanations of what may have given him the idea in the first place. Some have tried to make him out to be some kind of spirit-medium that spiritualists so often speak of, but the matter does not really gain the least in comprehensibility by this means.[2] On the other hand, what is more reasonable and natural than that a fifteen-year-old boy who had gone out

---

[a]. Compare Smith's autobiography.

[1]. It is interesting that in 1828 Joseph Smith took steps toward becoming a member of the Methodist church, eight years after his alleged first vision. For documentation, see *Mormonism: Shadow or Reality?* pp. 161-62.

[2]. Actually, there was a strong tie between Joseph Smith and the occult, as is documented in chapter 4 of *Mormonism: Shadow or Reality?* and *Mormonism, Magic and Masonry,* also by Jerald and Sandra Tanner (Salt Lake City: Utah Lighthouse Ministry). In fact, in 1826 Smith was tried and found guilty of the occult practice of peep stone gazing (see Wesley P. Walters, *Joseph Smith's Bainbridge, New York Court Trials* [Salt Lake City: Utah Lighthouse Ministry].

into the woods to pray should have fallen asleep and in that condition could have had a dream or such a vision as he relates. As to his emotions in the period immediately following he narrates the following: "Forbidden to join up with any of the sects of the day, and being very young in age, I was persecuted by those who ought to have been my friends and to have treated me with love. If they took me to be deceived, then they ought in love and in an appropriate manner to have tried to turn me back."

[p. 92] Shortly afterward Smith seems to have forgotten his high calling, as he according to his own confession fell into many kinds of vice and ungodliness. But in September 1823 as he was lying in bed he received a visit from an angel who told him the story about America's original inhabitants as well as about the golden plates and the place where they were buried. Yet it was not permitted him to receive the golden plates with the Urim and Thummim, and so on, until September 1827, when he received them from the angel's hands and straightway began the translation, with the assistance of Martin Harris and Oliver Cowdry. In 1830 the translation appeared in print under the title "The Book of Mormon." The period from 1823 to 1830 can be called the prophet's time of preparation. He was visited by John the Baptist, who ordained him as a priest, and later by Peter, James, and John, who appointed him an apostle. This was the first step toward the restoration of the priesthood and the Church. On April 6, 1830, the first Mormon congregation was founded, consisting of six people: namely, Joseph Smith, Sr., Hiram and Samuel Smith, Oliver Cowdry, Joseph Knight, and the Prophet himself. In the month of August in the same year Parley Pratt and Sidney Rigdon were converted to Mormonism. These men, both of whom were gifted Baptist or Campbellite preachers, gave to Mormonism its biblical and doctrinal development, and from that time on the new teaching began to develop. Missionaries were sent out, and many came to believe in the new prophet. In 1831 the Mormon society moved to Kirtland, Ohio, where Rigdon had won a number of proselytes, and in this city the first Mormon temple was built, which cost $40,000 and was completed in 1836. At its solemn dedication, attended by about a thousand saints, "the glory of the Lord filled the temple," and Moses and Elijah made their appearance before the prophet—so it is said by the scribes of the "Church" (although this is denied by others who were also present). In 1833 the management of the Mormon Society was given over to the so-called Presidency, consisting of Joseph Smith as President, with Rigdon and a certain G. Williams as Counselors. Not until 1835 was [p. 93] the so-called Quorum ordained, consisting of twelve "Apostles."

The Prophet continued constantly receiving revelations from heaven concerning the spiritual and earthly condition of the Church, and this along with a certain native cleverness is in all likelihood the reason that he personally, although surrounded by men who were far superior to him in learning and education, nevertheless continued to occupy the first place and the highest rank. But Joseph Smith is accused of having operated according to the principle that the shepherd should not only watch over his flock but also fleece it. Certain it is that he undertook many commercial enterprises which either lay beyond his horizon or which bordered upon criminality. In 1831, for instance, the "Kirtland Security Bank" was set up, which received the right to issue banknotes. These were ornamentally engraved with Joseph Smith's name as cashier and Sidney Rigdon as president. In the beginning they had a good sale, for no one expected that people who had daily meetings with the Lord Himself and with His angels could think of issuing banknotes without possessing capital to cover them. But the bubble burst, and some bankers in Pittsburgh sent a certain Mr. Jones to the Kirtland Security Bank in order to convert a large number of its banknotes into currency. Mr. Jones paid his respects to the president of the bank, Sidney Rigdon, and led off first with much expression of interest in the "Latter Day Saints" and the "progress of the good cause" in general. Sidney Rigdon felt very flattered by these inquiries, but when the pile of banknotes subsequently came to light, then the president of the bank took occasion to remark that Mr. Jones was conducting himself like "a wolf in sheep's clothing." The bank would not redeem these notes because to do so would be to harm it, and "the notes could be of use only as they circulated among the people." Mr. Jones made an offer that an exception to bank rules might be made in his favor, but Rigdon was completely adamant in this regard and gave him to understand that he would never have asked either him or anyone else to accept the notes. In conclusion he called his attention to that interesting [p. 94] point of time when the moneychangers were "driven out of the Temple in Jerusalem" with ridicule and scorn. Jones traveled back to Pittsburgh with his notes and the matter rested for a while, but afterwards the true state of affairs became known, and on January 12, 1838, the two bankers, Joseph Smith and Sidney Rigdon, had to take flight on horseback at midnight in order to avoid personal injury at the hands of their creditors. It was just like a new Mohammed's *hegira,* or "flight."[3]

This is how Kirtland became permanently impossible as a center for the new prophet and for the activity of his disciples. A new showplace had already been chosen and confirmed by a revelation to the prophet, who determined that a new temple and a new Jerusalem should be built up in Jackson County, Missouri, because that was where Paradise, or the Garden of Eden, was located, and it was there that Adam and Eve had walked face to face with their Creator. A new town was laid out on the north side of Grand River; the brethren called it "Spring Hill," but the prophet gave it the name of "Adam ondi Ahman"—which he interpreted as "The valley in which Adam blessed his children!" The city of Independence, which was renamed the New Jerusalem, was to be the capital of New Zion, and the saints were given orders to take the land around it into their possession! But it doesn't so easily come off in our days to take land into possession in a civilized state. The Mormons had neither money enough to buy land, nor strength enough to take it by force. They could only give assurances of their special selection by heaven and the rights which their hallowed status gave them in preference to others [who were]* ungodly heathen. But the latter would take no cognizance of such twaddle, and a series of conflicts arose, and they ended with the result that the people of Independence forced the saints to accept withdrawal from Zion and the New Jerusalem in the early part of 1834. When the information about this reached Kirtland, the prophet received a revelation which prompted

These words added for clarity.—Trans.

---

3. For a study of the Kirtland Bank Notes, see *No Man Knows My History,* chap. 14.

him to gather a small army of Mormons and at their head under the name of "Beurak-Ale" to march down to Missouri to destroy the ungodly and secure the rights of the saints. The prophet arrived during the middle of July [p. 95] in Clay County, Missouri, with his army, consisting of 205 men; there the people driven out of Independence had sought refuge. But those who had come to destroy were themselves destroyed by a plague of severe cholera which befell the prophet's camp and carried off many of his warriors. This circumstance, along with the fact that the "heathen" stood ready to receive the prophet [in battle],* evoked a new revelation in which he informed the army of Zion that this was a punishment for their not having heeded the word of the Lord, etc. With that the expedition came to an end. The prophet went back to Kirtland and New Jerusalem remained in the possession of the heathen. When Joseph Smith came back to Missouri after his flight from Kirtland, new disturbances soon arose once more, as might have been expected. Hostilities broke out on August 6, on an election day in Gallatin, Davis County. This was just a simple scuffle, but the hatred between the populace and the Mormons was already so intense that they soon resorted to weapons on both sides. The entire northern section of Missouri held its breath at the incredibly exaggerated rumors of bloody encounters with the Mormons, and the state governor, Bogg, had General Atchison march there with 400 militiamen, who later on were still further strengthened, in order to maintain order.

*These words added for clarity.—Trans.

On the twenty-third of October occurred the first encounter between the Mormons and the company of a certain Captain Bogart. In this the Mormons sustained three dead and nine wounded, whereas Bogart lost only one man; but nonetheless some maliciously minded persons took advantage of the circumstances to set the wildest rumors in motion. For example, it was related that Bogart's entire company had been massacred by the Mormons, whereupon Governor Boggs took occasion to issue an order that all the Mormons should either be destroyed or chased out of the state.

Such a cruel and ill-considered order to a population already highly aroused had of course the most lamentable consequences—as for example, the slaughter at Haun

Mills, in which eighteen or nineteen Mormon [p. 96] men, women, and children were murdered in the most shameful fashion by the enraged militia under the leadership of Captain Nehemiah Comstock.

It was not courage that Joseph Smith lacked; he still had desire enough to conduct open warfare with the heathen in order to avenge such injuries. But fortunately a man named Colonel Hinckle had command over the Mormon troops who were shut up within a little town called Far West, and in order to avoid bloodshed he took upon himself the moral responsibility of surrendering the Mormon leaders to the state troops when that had been specified as a condition for the establishment of peace. The prophet himself, Sidney Rigdon, Lyman Wight, Parley Pratt, and George W. Robinson were then placed before court martial and condemned to be shot; but to Missouri's honor one brave officer, General Doniphan, opposed the decision of the court martial and stated that neither he nor his brigade would be accomplices in a murder carried out in cold blood. In this way the lives of the Mormons were temporarily spared. They contented themselves with taking them as prisoners to Independence and later to Richmont in Clay County, where they were kept under heavy guard.

The majority of the rest of the Mormons received permission to return to their homes; but being constantly exposed to attack by the public and with those bloody injuries in their recollection, they gradually migrated to the State of Illinois under the leadership of Brigham Young, where the persecuted were granted shelter in a hospitable manner, and they offered them land in various localities. There also took place in a gradual way such a stark reversal in public opinion in Missouri regarding the Mormon disturbances that Joseph Smith and his fellow prisoners were allowed to leave jail, and soon afterward he made his appearance as a delivering angel among the Mormon migrants, who had located in large numbers in the town of Quincy, Illinois. A certain Dr. Galland thereupon offered the Mormons a large tract of land in Illinois between Burlington and Quincy, on condition that they settle down there. After looking the place over, the prophet accepted the offer.

[p. 97] An insignificant little town named "Commerce"

in the vicinity of the Mississippi River was selected as the headquarters of "New Zion," and it was renamed Nauvoo (which, according to Joseph Smith's "reformed Egyptian," was interpreted to mean "Lovely"), and this was now going to be the headquarters for the new Zion. By a new revelation through His servant Joseph, the "saints" were ordered to settle down there, and soon there arose a flourishing city flanked by well cultivated surroundings. The city of Nauvoo became incorporated and received its own charter from the Illinois legislative Assembly in 1840-41. Dr. J. C. Bennett, one of the prophet's favorites, was elected the first mayor of the city, and a militia force was set up under the name of "the Nauvoo Legion," over which Joseph Smith became "Lieutenant General." On April 6, 1841, the cornerstone was laid for a big new temple in Nauvoo with extraordinary pomp—as can be seen in the church's organ: *Times and Seasons*, which describes the proceedings in the following fashion:

> Early in the morning the announcement was given to Lieutenant General Smith that the Nauvoo Legion stood in readiness to hold a review. Led by its staff, consisting of four adjutants and twelve sergeants, almost all of them in gleaming uniforms, he made his way to the parade grounds. As he arrived he was greeted by the band with a fanfare of trumpets, and then it marched on in front of the General to the place which was reserved for him. The cannons were then fired again in his honor, and all the Legion saluted. It was indeed a splendid sight, the like of which had never been seen before and which is not expected to be seen again in the West. The various companies afforded a fine and interesting display, while the brilliant and expensive uniforms would have adorned a Washington or a Bonaparte.

Just imagine the Prophet, managing a high-spirited war-horse surrounded by such splendor! Look at him dismount from the proud beast in order to receive a new flag on behalf of the legion, fashioned by the hands of the most beautiful ladies! Then he hands it on to Major-General Bennet, the next in command, offering the vow to the ladies, "This flag shall never be dishonored [p. 98] so long as he is in command!" Anyone has to admit that Joseph Smith was a romantic just like a tragic actor on the stage. But at that time his good fortune stood at its zenith as well;

the various political parties recognized him and tried to secure his influence on their behalf. In February 1844, furthermore, the Prophet had the condescension, or the impudence—whichever you want to call it—to present himself before the American nation as a candidate for the Presidency, and he published a grandiloquent political address to the people in which he voiced his political views and set forth in bold strokes what glorious things could be expected if he should be elected. As noted earlier, Joseph Smith had a great sense of appreciation for the practical. Not only was he attracted to honor and titles, but also to the earthly blessings connected with them. Thus he received a revelation in Nauvoo on the 19th of January in which the Lord, among many other marvelous things, also commanded the saints to build a hotel that would be called "Nauvoo House," and it was to be built by the help of issuing stocks at a minimum price of $50, and they would not be higher than $15,000 per man, and, " 'Accord My servant Joseph a place in it from generation to generation, for I have put this anointing upon his head . . . therefore let Joseph and his seed after him have a place in this house forever,' said the Lord." At another passage in the same revelation it says: "Awake, ye kings of the earth! Come with your silver and gold to the help of My people to the house of the daughter of Zion!" The "saints" who lived in other localities received the following encouragement: "Come with your gold and your silver and all your antiques and all who have knowledge of antiques and such like. . . ." Of course Nauvoo House got built, and the prophet received a dwellingplace that was worthy of him. But the ruins of that building which still remain, that splendid temple and that flourishing city, are only like so many sorrowful commentaries on the Prophet's bombastic phrase "from generation to generation forever."

[p. 99] Joseph Smith became the first to tear down what he had built up, by his coming out with his foolish revelations about polygamy, for this created internal divisions among the Mormons and put them in a bad light before their neighbors. In another place we have discussed the doctrine of polygamy, and we shall confine ourselves to its effects upon the situation of the Mormons. The prophet conceived the idea of possessing himself of a woman married to William Law, the Major-General of the Nauvoo Legion, but the husband recognized injustice, and together with several of the most respected men of the city he formed a party to oppose the unlawful and despotic conduct of the Prophet. They obtained a printing press and published a paper, the *Nauvoo Expositor*, in order to set forth their views and unmask the Prophet, but only one issue of that paper ever came out. On April 6, 1844, the entire print shop was destroyed at Smith's command. Therefore the owners of the paper had the State order the arrest of the Prophet and his helpers, but the Nauvoo civil authorities had the order rejected and released the prisoners. This stupid move naturally increased the excitement on both sides, which now stood in armed opposition; and Smith's adversaries sent a committee to the governor of the State, Mr. Ford, to acquaint him with the affair. The governor himself took a trip down to Nauvoo, but when he arrived there, Joseph and his brother Hyrum had fled across the Mississippi to Montrose, Iowa, from which point he intended afterward to betake himself to Canada or to the Eastern States. But after receiving a letter from his wife Emma, in which she rather sharply let the two brothers know that they were "timid shepherds, who had left their flock as soon as danger was afoot," he decided to go back. Upon his return he was arrested and taken prisoner to the nearby city of Carthage, which was the county seat. This happened on June twenty-fourth, but on the twenty-seventh of the same month Joseph Smith and his brother Hyrum were killed in the Carthage jail by an armed and masked mob of men who had surrounded and taken possession of the jail.

[p. 100] From Governor Ford's own account of these events we set down the following:

> Convinced that the Mormon leaders had committed a crime by destroying the press of the *Expositor* and in opposing the exercise of lawful authority, I was determined to employ all the power of the State, if necessary, to bring them to obedience and to submission to the law. But when I found public opinion so aroused that there appeared to be a danger that it could degenerate into mob violence, I decided, before I proceeded to action, to secure the promise of the militia, officers and men, to support me in exclusively legal measures and to protect the prisoners if they should surrender . . . The assembled troops seemed to be very content with

my address and after I had finished, both the officers and the troops decided unanimously by acclamation to support me in exclusively legal matters and they promised that the prisoners would be protected against violence. It seemed to me that this vote justified me in promising the accused the protection of the law upon their surrender; and consequently they were appropriately advised at the same time that if they resisted, the power of the entire State would, if necessary, be summoned to compel them to subjection. A commando force* consisting of a constable and ten men was sent off to arrest them and bring the prisoners to headquarters. In the meantime Joseph Smith in his capacity of Lieutenant General declared the city of Nauvoo in a state of siege and called and Legion to arms [sic]. . . . Nauvoo was like a large army encampment and was so strongly guarded that no one could come out of the city and no one could enter in without being carefully searched. Nevertheless the constable upon his arrival was informed that the mayor and the council were willing to surrender and would appear in Carthage at eight o'clock the next day. Yet this promise was not fulfilled, for at that time Smith and Hyrum had fled to Montrose, and when the order of arrest was renewed the next day, the constable reported that the accused men were not to be found. . . . On the twenty-third or twenty-fourth of June, (continued [p. 101] the Governor,) Joseph Smith, who was also the mayor of Nauvoo, came along with his brother Hyrum, the members of the city council, and others who were involved. They came to Carthage and surrendered themselves as prisoners accused of insurrection, into the hands of the constable. All of the accused met voluntarily with the justice of peace, and were then released again, after they had obligated themselves to appear in court when their indictmant came up again with the exception of Joseph and Hyrum Smith, against whom the justice of the peace had drawn up an accusation of treason. . . .

*Or, "posse."
—Trans.

Immediately after Smith's arrest and at his own request I dispatched Captain Singleton and his company from Brown County to Nauvoo in order to take control of the city and take command of the Legion. Two hours after he had ordered the Legion to assemble for inspection, they assembled 2,000 strong in full armor, although the weapons of the State [i.e., the National Guard issue]* had been taken from them . . . Smith's hearing on the occasion of the charge of treason was deferred by the justice of the peace because none of the parties had any witnesses present. Therefore the accused were put in the county jail until later. . . . Neither they nor I had any serious apprehension that the prison

*These words added for clarity.—Trans.

would be seized by the guards who were stationed there to be responsible for them. All the less did it occur to me to worry that the prisoners might slip out, because such an attempt would simply have led to their instant death. . . . At that time there were twelve or thirteen hundred armed men in Carthage, and four or five hundred more in a city named Warsaw. All of them were eager to get into an expedition against Nauvoo, but upon Smith's surrender I had dismissed the militia with the exception of a small detachment who were stationed under the command of General Demming at the guarded prison in Carthage.

After that, (the Governor continued) I proceeded on my way immediately, [and]* accompanied Colonel Buckmaster and the company of dragoons under Captain Dunnis down to Nauvoo, which lies about 18 miles from Carthage. After we had covered four miles, Colonel Buckmaster called my attention to the fact he [p. 102] had an uneasy feeling that the prison might be attacked. This suspicion was based upon a secret conversation he had overheard between two persons. I myself had no presentiment about such an attack, for everyone in Carthage knew that we had decided to be away for a couple of days, and if anyone contested the arrest while we [were]* in Nauvoo, that would only have the effect of exposing my life and the life of my escort to the instantaneous revenge of the Mormons. However, in order to prevent a most unlikely episode, I sent back a company with direct orders to Captain Smith that under pain of death he should keep close watch over the prison until I returned.

*This word added for clarity. —Ed.

*This word added for clarity. —Ed.

The Governor and his entourage arrived at Nauvoo at four o'clock in the afternoon, where he summoned the citizens of the town together, and in an address he set forth to them the unlawful procedures of their leaders, and so on: ". . . Soon after sunset," the Governor continues,

we left the city behind and took our way toward Carthage. But a couple of miles outside of Nauvoo we met two men who told us that Smith and his brother had been murdered in the prison about five or six o'clock in the afternoon of the same day. This news appeared to us as positively stunning; I myself was completely amazed, and I foresaw the most serious consequences from this episode. I had the two men lead me back to Carthage as a precautionary measure to gain some time to come up with the necessary arrangements in case the Mormons might come seeking vengeance.[b]

b. Governor Ford's *History of Illinois.*

In Nauvoo the news spread sorrow and despair among the people during the following morning; a feeling of deep bitterness filled everyone's breast. To be sure, the two Apostles, Richard and Taylor, who had been present when the prophet was killed, had sent a letter to Nauvoo in order to calm the saints, as they admonished them to be calm and patient. The Governor dispatched a similar letter, in which he promised them his protection, but it was not likely that [p. 103] the Mormons trusted it, because the Governor had given the very same promises to the murdered prophet. On that afternoon of that same day the bodies of the slain arrived at Nauvoo. The mourning Mormons received them en masse and followed them to Nauvoo House, where the corpses were stationed until the necessary measures could be taken for burial which incidentally took place in all secrecy, in order to assure an undisturbed peace for the dead.[c]

It was in this tragic fashion that "the Prophet of the Nineteenth Century" brought his short but richly varied career to an end. In physique he was tall, powerful, and well built, and he had an especially attractive appearance. His nature was uninhibited and sociable, without being the least bothered in himself or before others as he put on a display of prophetic dignity. It is evident that he likewise possessed great natural—although misdirected—endowments.

Naturally it is difficult to determine how far his plans had extended themselves when he first began to perform the part of a prophet, but as the matter progressed step by step he perceived how deficient and inadequate his upbringing had been even for the work he had taken upon himself to carry out. Therefore he immediately began by setting up a school in the Kirtland temple, in which he himself was one of the most diligent students. Yet at the same time he knew how to maintain the highest rank both as a prophet and as a scholar. For none of the others had at their disposal that decisive "Verily, verily, thus saith the Lord. . . ," and no one else was gifted to translate "Reformed Egyptian" with the help of the "Urim and Thum-

---

c. It is a mystery even to this day where they interred the buried men. That is to say, it was rumored that for the advantage of scientific investigation, the prophet's head would be appropriated.

mim—God's gift and power." It is not without reason that the attempt has been made to compare Joseph Smith with Mohammed; and yet he showed that he rather had Moses [p. 104] as his model, for Mormonism turns out to be principally a reestablishment of the old Mosaic theocracy.[4]

Furthermore Joseph Smith knew as little tolerance as Mohammed toward the various Christian confessions of faith. The motto of the Arab was "The Koran or the sword!" and the American enjoined it upon his adherents to "take possession of the Land" whether by "money" or by "blood." Had they both had the same powers at their disposal and in the same situation, we would have seen about the same results. In order for Joseph Smith's mode of action to have been in consistent harmony with his line of thought, he may have reasoned about like this: "I have just as much right to found a new religion as Moses and Mohammed did, and to employ the same means to that end as they did." The same idea may be found also in the case of the freethinkers and spiritualists of our day, who, in case they believe in a "higher Being," always seem to solve the mysteries of faith by natural experiments and put animal magnetism, and so on, on a par with the operations and gifts of the Spirit of God, and furthermore they try to explain them by those means.

After the murder of the prophet and Hyrum Smith, the supreme power of Zion or the Mormon Church passed on to the Twelve Apostles, the president of whom was Brigham Young. Sidney Rigdon, who because of his rank stood next to the Prophet, was not only bypassed, but he was even excommunicated from the Church when he tried to assert his rights.

Rigdon had been Joseph Smith's right-hand man and the source from whom he had drawn his inspiration, but Brigham Young was determined to reap the fruits of harvest, and so on December 24, 1847, he had himself appointed President and supreme head.

---

4. Joseph Smith even compared himself to Christ and claimed to have outdone Him: "I have more to boast of than ever any man had. I am the only man that has ever been able to keep a whole church together since the days of Adam. A large majority of the whole have stood by me. Neither Paul, John, Peter, nor Jesus ever did it. I boast that no man ever did such a work as I. The followers of Jesus ran away from Him; but the Latter-day Saints never ran away from me yet" (*Documentary History of the Church,* 6:408-9).

Before proceeding further, we shall give a brief sketch of the new head of the Mormon Church.

Brigham Young was born in Whittingham, Windham County, Vermont on June 1, 1801. He grew up as a poor lad, and by his own admission, he received "only eleven and a half days of schooling." [p. 105] He learned the trades of glazier and painter, but he often served as an ordinary laborer for seventy-five cents a day. On April 14, 1832, he was baptized into "the Church of Jesus Christ of the Latter Day Saints,"[5] and shortly after that he moved to Kirtland, where he undoubtedly made great progress in his theological studies under the inspired leadership of the learned Rigdon and the eloquent Mr. Pratt. As for his religious views or "sentiments" (as he himself called them), he gives the following information: "Only one time did I ever feel any doubt or misgiving toward Brother Joseph Smith," but then he goes on to state that "this feeling did not last more than sixty minutes—or perhaps hardly more than thirty minutes." But Brigham tells how he very quickly regretted this error of his. "From that time on," he says:

> I never for a single moment believed that any man or any other human being in the whole world had anything to compare with him (i.e., Smith), for he was the supreme head over all, and he held the keys of salvation for them all. . . . He was God's servant, not mine, and he listened not to men, but to God, and if He should allow him (Smith) to lead the people into error or destruction, this would only take place because they deserved it. This was my belief, and still is.

From this quotation the readers can get a rather significant conception of the Mormon prophet's views and of his own prerogatives.

Joseph Smith as president and his brother Hyrum Smith and Sidney Rigdon comprised the highest authority in Nauvoo at the time when Joseph and Hyrum were murdered in the Carthage prison. Therefore Rigdon was the

---

d. Cf. the Mormon organ, *Journal of Discourses*, pt. four, p. 298.

5. The name of the church at that time was "The Church of Christ" (see footnote 1, chap. 1).

one who stood next to the office of prophet upon Joseph's death; but for some time he and his family had been living in Pittsburgh because of dissatisfaction with the Prophet, at whom he had been offended because he wanted his (Rigdon's) daughter as his wife.

[p. 106] After being advised of Smith's death he proceeded immediately to Nauvoo in order to take over the reins of government into his hands. But here he met with resistance. Brigham Young, who had arrived at the same time and had become the oldest in the apostolic office and therefore president of the quorum of the Twelve Apostles, now had Sidney Rigdon accused and summoned before the supreme council of the Church in Nauvoo. The charge against him was that he intended either to "rule or ruin the Church." The result of the hearing was that Rigdon, who was himself dissatisfied, was excluded from the Church. It states in the minutes, "Brigham Young arose and delivered him over to the punishment of Satan." And thus the way stood open for Brigham Young to power and greatness. Although Brigham's headship was immediately recognized by the great majority of the Mormons, it was not until December, 1847, that he was officially elected and recognized as President of the Mormon Church. Being untaught and uneducated himself, he was hostile toward scholarship and even up to the present he has successfully opposed the existence of a public school system for all of America. In personal appearance he is by no means repellant, and he has a fair and almost pleasant facial appearance and an expression of firmness and self-assurance. In his intercourse with others, both with his own large family and with strangers, his behavior is constantly distant and calculating, and he knows how to alternate between the role of a lion and that of a lamb. Practical minded and possessed of the speculative shrewdness native to Yankees, and of a conscience characterized by incredible elasticity, Brigham Young has, within the thirty years he has ruled over the Mormon Church, amassed for himself an almost incredible wealth, consisting of real estate both urban and rural, mills, factories, railroads, and so on, from which according to his own statements he receives a yearly income of "only $480,000"!* So that this modest flow of income may not depart from the Brigham dynasty upon his death he has for many years made an effort to have his

*And this in the economy of that day!—Ed.

son, Brigham Young, Junior, appointed as his successor in office as President of the Church. For this purpose Brigham Young had his three oldest sons secretly ordained as apostles by his own hands and those of the now deceased Heber C. Kimball[6] [p. 107] Yet it is rather unlikely that Brigham Young will attain his purpose in this regard.[7] It is more likely that upon his death the church will be divided into numerous sects and parties, each following its own prophet and leader. Of such there is in existence already now a very active party, under the leadership of the son of the murdered prophet—Joseph Smith, Jr., who call themselves the "True Latter Day Saints" or "Josephites," as contrasted with "Brighamites." These deny the doctrine of polygamy and even maintain that Joseph Smith never taught or practiced such a thing. There is however reason to suppose that Joseph Smith, Jr.,* along with others of the family, have in mind to defend and protect the name of the murdered man.[8]

*i.e., Joseph Smith III, the son of Joseph Smith, Jr., who founded Mormonism.—Ed.

The murder in Carthage had stirred up both the saints and the heathen to such an extent that the Mormons could no longer remain in Nauvoo, Illinois. Even the governor of the state could do nothing, despite all of his apparent efforts to effect peace and maintain the authority of the law in the face of the burning hatred which now flared up against the Mormons, even in cases where the law was on their side.

The people in the surrounding counties, who had "pledged their lives and honor" to drive the Mormons out, began to attack them and set their houses on fire and lay their property waste. As a consequence a supreme council consisting of the apostles of the Church and the leading elders held on January 20, 1846, decided that saints should leave the land and push out into the still uninhabited West. By February second they had already begun to prepare for the migration, and three days later the emigrants began to

6. Mormon scholar Stanley Kimball admits this in *Heber C. Kimball: Mormon Patriarch and Pioneer* (Champaign, Ill.: U. of Illinois Press, 1981), p. 294.
7. Brigham's son never became president.
8. Recently a document came to light that shows that Joseph Smith designated his son Joseph III to be his successor (see *Desert News*, March 19, 1981). Brigham Young himself seemed to acknowledge the fact that Joseph Smith's son would be involved in leadership in the Utah church (see *BYU Studies*, Winter 1976), pp. 223-30.

cross the still-frozen Mississippi River. By the end of the month about 1200 wagons had crossed over and were stationed on the west side of the Mississippi in the state of Iowa.

In the month of May about 10,000 pilgrims found themselves on their way through Iowa to arrive at a common meeting place by the Missouri River, the present Council Bluffs. In a petition which some of these emigrants presented [p. 108] to the governor of Iowa, their situation was described in the following fashion:

> . . . To stay is the same thing for us as to die by fire and sword, and to go into exile unprepared is the same thing for us as dying of hunger. And yet under these heartbreaking circumstances a few hundred of us have had to set forth on this painful migration and we are now camping in Lee County where we are suffering greatly from the piercing cold of winter. Some of us are already without food, others have provisions for just a few more weeks, and hundreds more will soon be following us in the same pitiable condition!

About a thousand Mormons had remained behind in Nauvoo, but it was by reason of poverty, sickness, and other circumstances which made it impossible to make the trip in this severe season; but the common rabble could not tolerate even these. In the middle of November about eight hundred men formed a mob and captured Nauvoo after a three days' siege. This proved to be the end of the great expectation and plans of the Mormons in Illinois.

The Prophet's lovely city, which once numbered about 15,000 inhabitants, became completely deserted; and the splendid temple, which was said to have cost a million dollars, now had become nothing but ruins!

On April 14, 1847, the first Mormons broke camp from their winter quarters at Council Bluffs and journeyed on farther west. By following the trail of General John C. Freemont's expedition, they reached the Valley of the Salt Sea on July twenty-third or twenty-fourth. The sight of this valley with its lake and rivers seemed like an irresistible inspiration to convince the weary and sorely battered pilgrims that this was the place where the Lord had decided for them to stay, in order to establish and fortify a new Zion for the third time.

The territory was formally taken into possession by Brigham Young, who like Joshua had led God's people into the promised land of Canaan. The deficiencies which the new prophet, both personally and from the romantic standpoint, might have in comparison with Joseph Smith, seemed now [p. 109] in full measure to be replaced by the natural superiority which the new Zion had over the former one—for here they had all the poetical scenery of nature that the ancient Mosaic prophets and singers speak of so beautifully. Soon the Mormon preachers and writings became so strongly inflated with expressions like "Zion's vales" and "Zion's mountains," etc., that anyone would feel assured that the American Zion up in the Rocky Mountains surpassed every other Zion in the world, and the "glad message" went forth even more full-blown than ever from "the Church of Jesus Christ of the Latter Day Saints" to the "benighted and fallen race of men." Missionaries were again sent out to proclaim the everlasting gospel. The saints came streaming into the new Zion from every quarter, cultivating the virgin soil, and as a rule they had a rich harvest. Thus it can be imagined how the Mormon colony soon enjoyed as flourishing a condition as ever before. Politically speaking, the Territory had earlier belonged to Mexico, but in July 1848, after holding a preceding convention, the Mormons sent off delegates to Washington with a request to Congress that Utah might be received into the Union. But it was not until November 9, 1850, that the United States* government would define its boundaries and appoint Brigham Young as governor and Indian commissioner, a dignity with which he was invested except for a brief, unimportant interruption until the early part of 1857, when James Buchanan was elected as president of the United States. In time there arose a general embitterment in the United States against the arbitrary illegality and intolerant despotism which prevailed in the realm of Brigham Young, where the teaching of polygamy and the absolutely insane doctrine of atonement by bloodshed (which we will discuss later) was publicly preached, as murder and contempt for the law was the order of the day. President Buchanan and his cabinet decided that the Mormons should be brought to respect the law, and as the first step in that direction an entirely new team of officials was appointed to govern Utah Territory. Alfred Cumming of Georgia was appointed as the future

*The original text reads "U.S."—Ed.

governor, D. R. Eckles became chief justice of their supreme court, John Cradlebough [p. 110] and E. E. Sinclair as associate justices, John Harnett as secretary of state, and P. R. Dotson as territorial marshal. A military force consisting of two regiments of infantry and a regiment of cavalry and two batteries under the command of General Harney were ordered to conduct the new governor to Utah in order to establish the authority of laws there. Van Vleit, the army quartermaster, who was sent on ahead in order to make arrangements for the accommodations for the troops, came to Salt Lake City in September, and was received by Governor Young with much courtesy. But at the same time it was made clear that although there was an abundance of everything that he required, yet nothing of this would be sold to the US Government and none of the soldiers who were now on their way to Utah would be given permission to enter the Territory. And he declared that if Governor Cumming came into the Territory, he *The original* [Brigham Young]* would put him in his coach and send *text reads* him back again. With this information Van Vleit left Salt *"B.Y."—Ed.* Lake City on September 14, and on the next day Brigham Young issued a proclamation for the citizens of Utah which concluded as follows:

> . . . I, Brigham Young, Governor and Superintendent for Indian Affairs in the Territory of Utah declare in the name of this people:
> 1) no armed force of any kind may enter this territory under any conditions whatever; 2) that all the armed men of the Territory shall hold themselves in readiness to march at a moment's notice in order to repel any hostile attack; 3) that this Territory is hereby declared to be in a state of siege. No person is allowed either to enter or to leave this Territory, unless he has obtained permission to do so from the proper authorities.

> Given under my hand and the Territorial seal
> on the 15th of September, A.D. 1857, and the
> 82nd year of the independence of the United States.
> Brigham Young.

A published proclamation was delivered to the commanding officer as soon as the first [p. 111] division of the governmental army reached the borders of Utah, with a mandate from Brigham Young to leave the Territory without delay by the same route as they had entered it.

On October fourth the Prophet's second councilor, who was likewise the top commander of the Mormon army, issued the following orders of the day:

> . . . Begin immediately to impede and harrass the army in every imaginable way just as soon as you have discovered their route and their present base. Make the utmost effort to drive away their draught animals and burn up their supplies and baggage wagons. Put to the torch the whole land both in front of them and on both sides of them. Disturb their night rest with nocturnal surprise attacks. Destroy access to the ferries wherever you can block their way by felling trees over them. Utilize every favorable opportunity to set fires on the windward side of their supply train, if it is possible to burn them up. And leave no grass behind which can be burned up in advance of them. Keep youselves hidden as well as you can, and don't allow youselves to be caught unprepared.
>
> Keep constant watch over the enemy by means of spies and keep in contact with Colonel Burton, Major McAlister and P. Rockwell, who are operating according to the same instructions. Inform me daily concerning their movements and every maneuver in whatever direction they may move.
>
> God bless you and give you success.
Your brother in the Lord,
Daniel Wells

These orders were literally obeyed. No less than three large transport trains with provisions, clothing, and tents were burned up, and their draught animals to the number of about 1300 were driven off to Salt Lake Valley as the "spoils of war." At the same time the winter was advancing, and whatever the Mormons could not steal or destroy now had to contend with hunger and cold. The army's line of march was constantly marked with dead and frozen beasts, and their encampment by "Black Forks," where 500 animals [p. 112] died at night between the sixth and seventh of November, well deserved its name of "Death Camp." Their position was virtually untenable, when Col. Sidney Johnston, one of the best US officers, arrived there with a small troop of reinforcements and took over the command of the "Utah Expedition." Since he saw no possibility of getting through the mountain passes until spring of the following year, he decided to go into winter quarters in the vicinity of a place called Fort Bridger, 150 miles from Salt Lake City. The expedition came to the new camp-ground, which received the name of Fort Scott, on the sixteenth of September after it had taken fifteen days to cover the thirty-five miles of distance from "Death Camp" by Black Fork to Fort Scott. The sufferings which General Johnston's army had to undergo in their winter quarters one can hardly imagine. The soldiers had to harness themselves to the wagons and drag firewood back to camp from the mountains while at the same time satisfying their hunger, when necessary, by eating the skins of dead animals. When Brigham found out that the army was suffering from a shortge of salt, he sent General Johnston a supply of this item as a gift, but the general contemptuously sent it back.

Meanwhile the Mormons were the happiest people under the sun. Their writings and songs from this period manifest a fanaticism and an arrogance that sounds almost incredible on the part of rational human beings! Yet Brigham Young was clever enough to forbid his warriors "to shed blood," and he restricted them to destroying the army by the stratagems of war.

In the long run the war would of course have ended with disaster for the "Saints," if a certain Colonel Kane from Philadelphia had not set about rescuing them from their dilemma.

Colonel Kane belonged to a very influential family and was himself a highly gifted man. On a trip to the West he had become acquainted with the Mormons during their expulsion from Nauvoo, and at that time he had probably sympathized with them in their sufferings. But that by itself scarcely furnished the basis of his strikingly overbearing procedure in the present case. There is an element of mystery still remaining, [p. 113] which we nevertheless should not try to explain, but merely recount the plain facts.

Kane went to President Buchanan and after a secret conference with him, he went by steamboat under the name of "Dr. Osborne" from New York to San Francisco, and from there went by land to Salt Lake City, where he arrived by the end of February 1858. The colonel had in his possession a document from Buchanan in which he stated that nothing but humanitarian considerations and a strong disposition to grant a service of mercy to the Mormon people could have moved him (Kane) to undertake such a mission (as to be peace negotiator) that was "so contrary to his own private interests." It is not known what secret correspondence or message Kane transmitted to Brigham Young, but its chief purport had undoubtedly been to promise the Prophet a pardon for all crimes committed up until that time, as well as to convince him of the hopelessness of waging war with the United States.

After negotiating with Brigham Young, Colonel Kane departed for General Johnston's headquarters at Fort Bridger, where he arrived on March twelfth and requested an audience with "His Excellency" Governor Cummings* without delay. This lack of etiquette in failing to announce himself first to the commanding general nearly involved the "humanitarian" colonel in a duel, had not Governor Cummings and Chief Justice Eckles known how to administer balm to General Johnston's wounded sensibilities. Colonel Kane concluded his mission with Governor Cummings as well in a very happy manner, for he had not only won the governor over to his plans, but he also managed to create bad blood between the governor and General Johnston, and since these two could of course accomplish something only in mutual cooperation, the war really came to an end at that juncture.

*The spelling of the governor's name with an s from this point forward is in the original Danish.—Trans.

On April third "His Excellency" Governor Cummings advised General Johnston that he was now ready to proceed to Salt Lake City in order to assume [p. 114] control of his office as Governor of Utah.[e] Two days later he left Fort Scott in the conduct of the diplomatic colonel.

As soon as they were beyond General Johnston's military lines, a Mormon detachment of guardsmen received them with military honors, and during the entire tour to Salt Lake City the Mormon militia greeted the new governor as if he had been their own victorious champion, or triumph-

---

e. As soon as the Mormons had recognized Cummings as Governor of Utah, he also had supreme command over all the troops in the Territory. General Johnston therefore could not accomplish anything but in accordance with Cummings's orders. The end result of this large and costly Utah Expedition was a wretched farce.

ing leader, as a "mighty man of the kingdom." And also as soon as he arrived at Salt Lake City on April twelfth, a grand reception was made for him, and "His Excellency the Ex-governor Young was not among the last" [to greet him].*

Meantime President Buchanan had appointed two commissioners who were to travel to Salt Lake City and offer to Brigham Young and his accomplices an unconditional pardon, provided they laid down their arms and submitted to the United States. On June seventh the commissioners arrived in Salt Lake City, and Buchanan's pardon was accepted by the mighty Prophet and his apostles.ƒ But in order to grant General Johnston and the troops he had brought with him some sort [p. 115] of formal satisfaction, they were allowed to stage a sort of parade-march through Salt Lake City's avenues. The city was quite forsaken, incidentally, because over 30,000 Mormons had fled from Salt Lake to Utah Valley, from which they returned when they saw that no seizure of their person or property would take place. This flight seems to confirm the old proverb: "The wicked always fear"! The troops later set up camp a few miles from Salt Lake City by the Jordan River, where they remained inactive until the conflict between the Northern and Southern States called them back.

And so this is the way the war between President Buchanan and the prophet Brigham Young came to an end. The great Utah Expedition, which cost the United States many millions of dollars and the lives of many men, produced only meager results and little honor for the nation. Brigham Young and the Mormons were enriched by the immeasurable booty and the commissary supplies which the Expedition had brought into their hands; and the

ƒ. In September 1856 Brigham from his speaker's throne in the Tabernacle had communicated to the people the following proud declaration in regard to the prospects for himself and for his kingdom: "I say unto you, as truly as the Lord lives, so long shall we remain an independent state in the Union—or else an independent state for ourselves!—I am now Governor of this Territory and shall so remain, and that too in the face of the constant malice and vexation of my enemies, who have always occupied themselves with demonstrating against me." Then the inspired prophet continued, "Twenty-six years will not elapse before the elders of this Church will be as highly esteemed as kings upon their thrones" (Deseret News).

Prophet, although he was no longer "governor" of Utah, nevertheless remained the supreme autocrat over the Mormons despite the laws of the United States and of the Territory.

9 Secret Mormonism

[p. 116] Behind the Mormonism as it shows itself to us there lies a secret, hidden organization which more than anything else has brought about the practical consequences which the Mormons have attained and which they will gladly cite as an evidence of the divine veracity of their doctrine. So long as we are not in a position to raise the curtain on this secrecy, which from the very beginning has made up one of the chief ingredients of Mormonism, the progress made by this entire teaching and the procedures of its leaders will remain basically incomprehensible to us. It can be easily seen that people in foreign regions of the world, unacquainted with the true nature of Mormonism and its history, can allow themselves to be ensnared and for a time to give many evidences of true devotion for the sake of the faith. But that same people after living in Utah and learning of the revolting deceptiveness [that goes on there],* should not only continue to profess Mormonism, but even to all appearances continue to offer themselves up for the sake of the faith, as they oftentimes forsake home, wife, and children without compensation in order to go to foreign lands as missionaries— this will remain inexplicable to us so long as we do not

*These words added for clarity.—Trans.

realize that to these people (who very often bear symbols upon their bodies that make them dependent upon the will of their leader and constantly remind them of the great and all-embracing dogma) Obedience—blind and unconditional obedience—is the first and great commandment on which hang the Law and the Prophets in the State of Brigham Young. The good missionaries of Zion as a rule are simply not asked about their faith or desire to go forth as missionaries, but they simply take orders from their lord and master, Brigham Young, to go forth and [p. 117] "fish for men" in this or that part of the world, and they obey. There are even examples given to the Prophet's having sent people on a mission in order to punish or ruin them, and nevertheless they have not ventured to refuse to go. But the purpose of sending people out may of course be a good one as well, for the Prophet is a father to his people. Thus in 1853 he sent forth his own son and the sons of his two counselors to England, so that the three young princes of the Church might be reformed and acquire a taste for fishing for men, instead of holding nocturnal feasts in Salt Lake City in honor of Bacchus—though much to the vexation of the "saints" and the Prophet. This obedience holds good, of course, in all situations. If Brigham orders one of the saints to go out and kill some apostate, nine times out of ten he will carry out the murder, in all probability. Who can believe, for instance, that even half of the Mormons who took part in the "Mountain Meadows Massacre" did so on a free impulse of their own? Doesn't that bloodhound Bill Hickman say himself in his confession, that the murders he perpetrated were in accordance with his orders? One might of course raise the question of how these men, who in many cases were born and brought up under entirely different conditions, could have subjected themselves to such degrading spiritual slavery. Well, this is a profound and difficult question to explain in a basic way. As much as we can determine, it is a gradual process. It comes to mind that an English poet, Pope, explains the stages in a rather striking way when he states in his "Essay on Man":

> Vice is a monster with such a frightful mien
> As to be hated needs but to be seen;
> But seen too oft, familiar with its face,
> We first endure, then pity, then embrace.*

*Ahmanson, having quoted this quatrain in English, proceeds to render it into Danish in this footnote.— Trans.

[p. 118] Nor is there anything quite so strange as the opinions, or more accurately, the foundations, upon which they are based. What is regarded today as sinful and wrong may perhaps a few years later be regarded as a perfectly correct and allowable thing. The old theories about conscience or the voice of God within us seem to be exclusively due to external influences or the force of habit. For certain cannibals feel no pangs of conscience in eating their dead parents. Likewise the Indian, when he steals or robs all that he can manage—indeed, the more scalps he obtains, the more esteemed he is. The ancient Norsemen felt very pricked in conscience when they failed to carry out blood vengeance that was incumbent upon them. But by frequent wielding of the sword and the slaughter of as many enemies as possible was what made one worthy to share in the joys of Valhalla. The Catholic regards the matter of his salvation to be assured against all danger if he remains in the bosom of the pope or the salvation-bringing church, whereas the Quakers on the other hand feel assurance on the basis of their own inner purity. Hence the moral and religious concepts of men are not innate gifts of nature but are exclusively the products resulting from the influence of external favorable surroundings.

So it is when the honest and naive European proselyte first arrives in Utah and comes to find out how things really are, he most usually shudders at them, but considering his own helplessness he is by and large forced to put up with them. Then if he does not possess enough moral and physical courage to break away from it while there is still time, then time will alter the relationships and invest them with a new appearance in his eyes. Then partly under compulsion, partly with an attitude of indifference, he follows along with the mainstream, until the moment comes when the authorities of the Church deem it wise to have him initiated into "the secrets of the Kingdom," which in connection with polygamy plunge him for good into the abyss of secret oaths, covenants, and signs that make up the secret level of Mormonism and which are shared with a candidate in Utah under the label of "gifts from on high." Not until then is he regarded as standing in full fellowship with the Mormon Church in Utah.

[p. 119] As I deal with the present theme I should first observe that although I myself did not go through this mystical rite while I, as said before, was holding aloof from sharing in the Mormon organization during my stay in Utah, nevertheless there were many kinds of things which even then convinced me of the true nature of this "endowment." That is to say, while I was living in Salt Lake City, a small pamphlet fell into my hands discussing this subject, published by a married couple named Van Dusen, to the best of my recollection, and confirmed with an oath. It had small woodcut illustrations that presented the same scenes of "Creation," "Washing," "Anointing," and so on, as Elder John Hyde describes in his book *Mormonism*, which did not come out until a year later.

John Hyde, from whose book I have taken the following description, was a gifted and well-informed young Englishman who migrated with his father to Utah in 1853. Like so many others he soon discovered that it was far from being the "promised" Zion. In 1853 he was sent as president of a mission society to the Sandwich Islands, and it was during his trip there that he summoned up the courage to pass judgment against the doctrine which he had believed in since the age of fifteen. Upon his arrival in the Sandwich Islands he stated his opinions to the other members of the mission concerning this matter, and he began to give lectures there and later on in California. When he had published his book, *Mormonism*, he journeyed back to England, where he is now a respected clergyman. I was personally present in the Tabernacle on January 11, 1857, when the prophet Heber C. Kimball read aloud two letters which had come in from Hyde's colleagues in the Sandwich Islands. These letters seemed to inspire this "Abu Bakr" of Mormonism with an almost fanatical enmity. He made a motion, which was seconded by the third dignitary of the Church, D. Wells, that John Hyde be "cut off" from the Church of Jesus Christ of the Latter Day Saints and be turned over to the power of Satan, and so on.

In a letter to Brigham Young dated "New York, July, 1857" Mr. Hyde expressed himself in the following manner:

> [p. 120] I have revealed the mysteries connected with your secret order and its treacherous oaths, and I have done so, not in order to satisfy any extreme public curiosity, but

to show your adherents outside of Utah what plans there are which are set forth for their support and assistance, and what kind of blessings they are which you maintain that God has saved up for them there. I have done this also in order to draw the attention of the U.S. government to the true purpose and nature of your system. . . . I feel that both God and my reason fully assent to my violating these secret oaths, and I feel equally justified in breaking my oaths of obedience. I am fully aware that in so doing I expose myself to the punishment which you have tied in with those obligations. But I believe that my duty is even greater than the danger which may pursue me. If your doctrine is true, it does not need to fear the light of day; if on the other hand it is false, then both you and the human race in general will gain benefit from its being known and understood [as such].* I must confess that in my opinion you are relying sincerely upon (the special) election of Smith and of yourself as well, but it is evident that you are at the same time leading thousands of trusting souls to ruin and destruction. A feeling of sympathy for them is also one of my incentives for frustrating your plans. . . .*a*

These words added for clarity.—Trans.

Now we should like to pass on to John Hyde's account of how he received "the endowment from on high."

. . . Much has been said about the bestowment or "Endowment" of the Mormons. Those who have received or gone through these mysteries have always tried to present them as something extraordinarily great and exalted, to the point that people really supposed that there was something sublime about them. Those who were in possession of the secrets, because of their pride in them, and out of a desire for everyone to have an idea of their advantages, have occasionally let a few obscure hints slip out. [p. 121] Thus they have displayed some peculiar undergarments bearing mystical sign, which they received in the Temple and which they constantly wear. They related to their amazed hearers that this endowment was full of the heavenly bestowments, and so on. . . but what it was in reality or what it consisted of remained a deep secret, for which anyone who had gone through the mysteries would be visited with fearful punishment should he ever reveal any of them.—Oaths were required which obligated the person concerned to take upon himself liability for a sudden and violent death, should he

---

a. Cf. *Mormonism* by John Hyde.

ever reveal the mysteries. I am now about to give an account of these ceremonies as well as I can remember them, and the following reasons move me to break by oath:

1) Since no one knew of the contents of these oaths until he heard them, and since no one after hearing them dared to deny or reject them, they are from the legal standpoint of no binding force. 2) These vows include obedience as well; but since I have no more intention to obey, therefore it can no more be unfitting for me to break a promise of silence than the promise of unconditional obedience. 3) These obligations include treason toward the United States, and are therefore illegal. Furthermore, since the law regards concealment of treason as equivalent to treason itself, it becomes a duty to reveal the same. 4) Since the promise of this endowment is one of the most important enticements to impel Mormons to migrate to Utah, it is reasonable for them to be acquainted with the true value of these expected blessings. 5) It is better to break a sinful promise than to keep it. Thus it would have been better for Herod to break his promise than to kill John the Baptist.

In regard to the punishment which I bring upon myself, inasmuch as my only obligation is to God and the world at large, I therefore place my security in God and the world, as well. On Friday, November 10, 1854 my wife and I, after previous instruction, went to the Endowment House in Salt Lake City, where we met with thirty other people who were waiting there and who like us were to receive the bestowment from on high. Our names, our dates of birth, the date of our wedding, and so on, were inscribed in a book, [p. 122] and our receipts from the Office of Tithes were examined—for before one hears the music he must pay the musicians. Those of us who were not previously *sealed* unto our wives were now sealed by Heber C. Kimball, whose special business it was to impart the bestowment. Then we were taken into a long room which was divided into several smaller rooms by various white drapes. The ladies were [assigned]* to one section of the house and the men to another. Everything was solemn and hushed; not a word was spoken except by the officiating ministers in a soft, whispering tone.

*This word added for clarity. —Trans.

One after another was called in, and after a while it was my turn. I got undressed when ordered to do so, and then I was put down into a large bathing pool made of tin, but painted over both inside and out. A Dr. Sprague, who incidentally is one of the most crude and vulgar people I have ever seen, performed the service of washing, which ceremo-

ny consisted of getting washed with lukewarm water over
the entire body from head to toe, while an appropriate
blessing was pronounced over each part of the body—such
as over the brain, that it might remain strong, and over the
ears, that they might be quick to hear God's word, and so on.
After I had been washed and declared free from the blood of
this generation, I was turned over to Parley Pratt, who was
sitting in a corner to give each pure man a new name by
which he would be known in the Kingdom of God. He called
me "Enoch." Then we were led back to the first room,
where we all were seated on chairs and a strongly scented
oil was held over our heads from a vessel of mahogany in the
form of a horn of plenty. Our eyes, ears, nose and mouth
were in the meantime being smeared with this ointment,
until we felt well greased and very fragrant. The anointing
was taken care of by two elders, Taylor and Cumming. And it
was carried on with a series of blessings similar to those
which were employed during the washing. The ceremony of
anointing was a preparatory step toward ordination as
"King and priest unto God and the Lamb"—a ceremonial
consecration which can, however, only be carried out in the
actual [p. 123] temple.[b] Having been thus anointed and
blessed, we had to put on some new clothes ("the garments") made of muslin or linen. They had to be worn next
to the body; they reached from the head to the feet and
incidentally they resembled the nighttime pajamas of an
infant. A shirt was put on over this, and on top of that again
a linen jacket that reached to the neck and hung loose over
the one shoulder and was equipped with a belt around the
waist. A cap made of a cubit of squared linen wrapped
together so that it fitted around the head. The costume was
completed with stockings and white linen shoes. While we
were being thus costumed, a farce was being performed in
the adjoining room which was supposed to represent "the
Creation." In it "Elohim" took counsel with "Jehovah," Jesus, and Michael concerning the populating of earth, and
they sent down the three last named to bring back a report
of the prospects. They go and come back again, and with
this the first chapter of Genesis is completed. Elohim is "the
Lord"; He is the one who speaks when it says: "The Lord
said," etc. The other three carry out His commands and they
say: "And there was light," etc. This entire comedy gave the
impression of being a silly spoof of God. At the conclusion of

b. This expensive temple which the Mormons are so eager to erect
   resembles a heathen temple more than Christian churches or
   meetinghouse.

the farce Jehovah, Jesus, and Michael came down to us in order to carry out the work of the sixth day, or the creation of man, which proceeded with the touching of our bodies and blowing into our faces, and so on.

We were now assumed to be, like Adam, newly created and completely obedient and malleable in God's hands (an allegory which was soon to become a reality in a fearful way), but we were "alone." And yet—after a little more comedy—our wives were brought in. They wore clothes just like us, and they had gone through the same ceremonies. Of course this service had been carried out by women, Miss E. R. Snow and some others. [P.124] We were now commanded to shut our eyes and pretend to fall asleep, and at the command, "Arise and see!" our wives were given back to us. Happiness filled our hearts, of course, and thus we had to march two by two into the room from which we had heard the voice of Elohim. With the help of a few small spruce trees, etc., this room was supposed to represent Paradise.

W. C. Staines and Miss E. R. Snow played Adam and Eve, and we were supposed to imitate everything they did. Some raisins (which were of course supposed to have been apples) were hanging from a bush, and W. W. Phelps, who represented Satan (and he played the role in an outstanding fashion) tried to get us to eat them. Of course the woman tempted me and I ate. But then we were cursed by Elohim, who came looking for us. Satan was chased away, and that learned astronomer and apostle crawled away on his hands and feet whistling and hissing.

After that we were regarded as fallen and lost creatures, and now began the serious and fearful part of this otherwise so foolish performance.

From our fallen and helpless condition we could be rescued only by a higher power and a higher law: but this power and this law was given by God as He established the priesthood, on which He bestowed the needful authority. Its power was boundless, its commands were beyond contradiction, its judgment was unshakable, and its authority was unsurpassed.

The priesthood became God's vicarious substitute; it was to act with God's authority and in God's stead. Oaths of inviolable silence, of obedience, of dependence upon the priesthood, and especially of not touching any woman unless she were given him by the priesthood—these oaths were now read out by the president to the semi-initiated and intimidated neophytes. A symbol, a special handshake and a password were now imparted and impressed upon our

memory, and thereby the third degree of Mormon endowment—or the first stage of Aaron's priesthood—was imparted to us.

Man—as the allegory continues—now goes forth into the
world, in which darkness is light and light is darkness. He
roams about in uncertainty as to what is [p. 125] right, as
he has only a lesser law and a lesser priesthood to be led by.
In this way we entered a room where we were assumed to
be in the midst of the sects of our own time, and where
various representatives of the sects of our era were exhibit-
ed, such as Quakers, Methodists, and so on. Satan (W. W.
Phelps) meets and greets each of them with, "Good morning, Brother Methodist," etc. "I love you all, you are all my
friends." But then he encounters three Apostles, Peter
(P. Pratt), James (I. Taylor), and John (E. Snow), who
disturb the good relationship between the "Old" (Harry) and
the sects. After a bit of squabbling between him and the
Apostles, Peter finally commands Satan to "be gone, in the
name of the Lord Jesus Christ and by the authority of the
holy priesthood," and Satan exits in a frightful rage!—Now
the three Apostles begin to investigate our situation, and
they give us new instructions, not only in regard to the
priesthood in general as an abstract idea, but also in regard
to the princes of the Mormon Church, as the unique representatives of the priesthood.

The purpose of all this was to show how the three Apostles
named came down to Joseph Smith and imparted the priesthood to him, which passed from him to Brigham Young. All
the reverence which otherwise would be accorded to Christ
and the Apostles consequently belonged to the Mormon
priesthood now. To it one must manifest an immediate, unconditional obedience, and be (as Kimball said) "like a
greased rag in the hand of Brigham Young!" Now we are,
according to the allegory, on our way to the Kingdom of
God! God has had compassion on the fallen world and revealed His Gospel to Smith, upon whom He has bestowed
the priesthood. But God now requires unconditional obedience as well toward Smith and his successors. The punishment for breaking the oath of silence on the part of the first-
degree Mormon would be that his throat should be cut; in
the case of a second-degree Mormon, his heart should be
ripped out—and so on down the line, set forth in gruesome
detail, for now the farce had passed over into fearsome
reality.

All the rank of neophytes finished up with a new symbol, a
handshake [p. 126] and some passwords. The allegory now

presents man in a partially saved condition. We are conducted into another room with an altar in its center. Here we are pledged to unbroken fidelity to the brethren, and in particular, never to speak ill of the Lord's anointed—or in other words, to keep our mouths shut in regard to any crime of theirs whatever—to see but not to speak. We should not only think with their thoughts and feel as they feel, and act as they act, but also we should go to them as mediators between Christ and mankind, just as Christ is the Mediator between them and God. And finally, we are to show unconditional obedience to every command, however treasonable, criminal, unnatural, or unspiritual it might seem.

We are to keep the Church foremost in our thoughts and offer to it our exclusive devotion. We are to be constantly ready to sacrifice our warmest friend, our nearest relative, our dearest wife, yea even our own life and blood—and keep nothing whatever in our possession as sacred, or keep any oath as binding which might in the slightest way oppose or hinder the interests of the Church.

After this oath was taken, we received a new symbol with a handshake and a password, and thereby we had attained the first degree in the higher of Melchizedek-level priesthood. The punishment for transgressing or revealing this oath would be to have one's navel cut out and to be disemboweled, etc., etc., elaborated on in every frightful and abhorrent way possible.

Speechless, fatigued, and bowed down with a feeling of a frightful, unnatural responsibility, and trembling with a kind of presentiment as to what might still be in store, we were conducted into the next room. Here an altar stood in the midst, and on it lay the Bible, the Book of Mormon, and Smith's Revelations (the Book of the Covenant). Both men and women among us were stationed around this spot. Kimball stood near us. Brigham in the next room was also watching. Parley P. Pratt officiated, and the fourth oath was read aloud. The allegory now presumed that men were on a tolerably secure pathway to salvation, but for the time being they had a solemn duty to fulfill. This was no abstract theory about [p. 127] obedience, nor even obedience in certain abstract situations, but a vital and stringent obligation. We had to swear to cherish an abiding hatred toward the government of the United States, because it had not avenged the death of Joseph Smith or done anything in regard to the "persecutions" of the "saints." We had to swear to do everything we could to bring down and unsettle this government, and try to disrupt its plans and frustrate its purposes. We were to renounce all loyalty and refuse all submission to it. If we should be ourselves unable to achieve anything along this line, we should inculcate this principle in our children.[1] And on our deathbed we should bequeath it to them as our final wish, which would be the holiest duty of their entire life and their dominating thought—to the end that the Kingdom of God and Christ (the Mormon hierarchy) might subject to itself all other kingdoms, until it should cover the earth! The most frightful curses and the most barbaric punishments were presented as the prospect for those who did not observe these particulars or who dared to reveal them. A new sign and handshake and a password—and a second degree of the Melchizedek priesthood was imparted. Now we would, according to the allegory, be acceptable to God and come to Him as His child. But we were told that our outer jacket was hanging on the wrong shoulder and as a sign of our dependence on the priesthood, they took it and placed it on the right shoulder.

In order to bestow on these actions a more profound religious form, they taught us now a new mode of prayer. We were all placed in a circle that we might repeat all those symbols, and so one, in a soft tone, which had been part of the bestowment formulas, and thereupon our hands and arms were linked together in a fanatical way. As we were positioned in that fashion, one who was assigned to do this fell upon his right knee, took hold of the hand of his nearest brother, and then prayed slowly, while everyone in the circle repeated his words.

This kind of praying is regarded as especially potent with God. Brigham and the twelve apostles often pray after this fashion, partly in order to repeat and recall the appointed symbols, and so on.

On this occasion it was Parley P. Pratt who was [p. 128] the officiating priest [who prayed]* that "God would curse or bless us in the same proportion as we obeyed or neglected this covenant into which we had entered" and that which he had prayed we had to repeat after him word for word.

*These words added for clarity.—Trans.

By these means we would be brothers and members of the holy order of the priesthood of the Lord, and we would have access to all the glories of this brotherhood. We could show recognition of each other at any time; monstrous mysteries bound us together, and we were connected to the priesthood by frightful oaths.

---

1. This oath of renunciation has since been removed from the temple ceremony. For a study of the temple ceremony, see *Mormonism: Shadow or Reality?* chap. 29-32.

We were now to pass beyond the "curtain" (a curtain of white linen) and at the same time we were to repeat all the previous formulas. Then a pair of identifying marks were cut into the front of our shirts and another name was whispered to us, but in such a hurried and lowered tone that it was difficult to make it out. Thus we walked through the curtains into "the Heavenly Kingdom of God"; after that we went back and let our wives in, who had to repeat the same formulas. In "the Heavenly Kingdom" were Brigham and several others, who were waiting to hear the "endowment lectures" which were delivered on such occasions.

We received permission to put on our clothes, and since it was four o'clock already, we enjoyed a few refreshments— also in haste—after which we proceeded back to the "Heavenly Kingdom" to hear a lecture. This was delivered by H. C. Kimball, who in the course of it explained further the profound and serious significance of the allegory, and repeated the secret symbols already given, as well as all the formulas, so as to impress them on our memories, since these symbols are necessary for recognition by another initiate. This all ended with some frightening, very significant threats. When it was six o'clock we all went back to the assembly room, where we put on our own wardrobe again, and thus the affair was brought to a close. "There are but few men," says Hyde, "who have the strength of character or the courage sufficient to throw off the stupefying impression, or overcome the influence upon the mind, which the experience of such a day leaves behind!"

No better proof of this is given than the [p. 129] recognition of the fact that out of the many hundreds of those who like John Hyde had gone through this pandemonium but who later forsook and denied Mormonism, not one (so far as I know) has ever ventured to reveal and declare what it is. That the reasons which Mr. Hyde presents for his own disregard of these vows and covenants are good and sensible, certainly no right-thinking person will deny. I have repeated his revelation here because there are undoubtedly thousands of my compatriots in Utah who, although they have received the so-called endowment, nevertheless because of their ill acquaintance with the English language are still comparatively unaware of the true significance and character of this "endowment." In the hope that these too might come to see that a Society which has to hide itself in the dark cannot be from Him who is the Light and the Father of light this is my motive for bringing this all out here into the open.

10 The Danites

[p. 130] In addition to—or perhaps in connection with—the odious system of the "endowment," Mormonism has a second band of conspirators, the so-called Danites, or "destroying angels." It is a gang of out-and-out murderers, who at certain times have given rise to considerable suspicion and in some places great fear. The presence of the Danites can be demonstrated already from the sojourn of the Mormons in Missouri back in 1838, as may be seen from the following sworn testimony of Thomas B. Marsh, (who at that time was president of the Twelve Apostles), and also of Orson Hyde, the current president of the Apostles in Salt Lake City:

Thomas Marsh's Testimony

They had among them an organization regarded as consisting of trustworthy Mormons which was called "Danites," and these men had given their oath to support the leaders of the Church in all things, whether right or wrong. Yet some of the organization are dissatisfied with this oath, which they regard as conflicting with moral and religious principles. Mormons have told me that in Far West last Saturday a group of twelve men was chosen that goes by the name of "the Destroying Band." It was decided that if any people from Buncombe come to inflict harm and destruction upon the people in Caldwell (who were Mormons), then this band would set Buncombe on fire; and if the inhabitants of Clay and Ray make any move against them, then the Destroying Band will burn up Liberty and Richmond.

*i.e., Missouri.—Ed.

[p. 131] It is the plan of the prophet Joseph Smith to take possession of this State,* and he assures his people that it is his purpose to conquer the United States and in the end, the entire world. I believe that these are the prophet's plans and purposes, just as it is the belief of the Church (itself). It is the teaching of the prophet and the faith of the people, that his revelations are superior to the laws of the land. I have heard the prophet say that he would yet tread his enemies down and walk over their dead bodies; and that if they did not leave him in peace, he would become a second Mohammed to this generation, and would make this country into a sea of blood from the Atlantic Ocean to the Rocky Mountains. Just as Mohammed motto was: "The Koran or the sword!", so it would become "Joseph Smith or the sword." These last statements were uttered last summer. The number of armed men in "Adam Ondi Ahman" (the then existing Mormon Zion) was between three and four hundred.

Thomas B. Marsh
Sworn to and signed in my presence.
Richmond, Missouri, October 24, 1838.
Henry Jacobs
Justice of the Peace, Ray City, Missouri

*These words added for clarity.—Trans.

"I know [for certain]* that the greater part of the preceding disclosures are true, and I believe that the rest is true as well.

Sworn to and signed.
Richmond, Missouri, October 24, 1838.
Henry Jacobs
Justice of the Peace, Ray City, Missouri

[p. 132] To this is added a certificate on the part of seven persons residing in Ray County, who testify that Marsh was President of the Twelve Apostles, and Orson Hyde was one of the Twelve, and that they have now left the Church on the ground of the Mormons' immoral and ungodly behavior.

The honor of having first organized and trained this secret band of murderers goes to a certain Dr. Alvord, who at that time was one of Joseph Smith's disciples. In a speech delivered to this chosen society concerning the greatness of the coming kingdom, he concludes in the following way:

> My brethren, you have been chosen to become our leading men, our captains to rule over this Church of Jesus Christ, which has now been organized after the ancient order. I have gathered you this day to teach and instruct you in the things that pertain to your duties, and to make perfectly clear to you what your prerogatives will soon be. Don't you see, brethren, that it will soon be your privilege to go forth with your various companies and wage war against the boundaries of the settlements and take plunder from the ungodly heathen? For it stands written: "The kingdoms of the heathen shall become hallowed to My people, which is the house of Israel." And in this way you shall devastate the heathen by robbing and plundering their possessions. It is in this way that God intends to establish His Kingdom in these last days. If anyone of you should be discovered, who is able to harm us? For we will stand together and defend one another in everything. If our enemies conspire against us, we can conspire as well.[a] How is this? You seem to be frightened at this, brethren. As truly as the Lord lives, so truly I would swear to a lie, in order to rescue any of you whoever; and if I couldn't do so, then I would bury him or them in the sand, just as Moses did with the Egyptian! In this way we shall greatly sanctify the Lord and upbuild His Kingdom. Who can stand against us? If any of us should be found to have transgressed, then we would deal with him among ourselves. And if any of this Society of Danites reveals any of these things, then I will hide him in a place where no dog will be able to gnaw at him. . . .

[p. 133] The name "Danites" is taken from Exodus 49:17* where it says: "Dan shall be like a serpent on the way, like an arrow-snake upon the path, that bites a horse in his heel, so that his rider falls backward!" In the beginning incidentally they were called "the sons of Dan," but their program was carried out in such a way that[b] "many men have fallen backward, never more to arise or to be seen again."

*A misprint for Genesis 49:17.— Trans.

---

a. The captains appear to have become a bit confused at this point— an observation of the Mormon Church's own chronicler.

b. Cf. *Mormonism* by John Hyde.

It did little good for Joseph and the Mormons to attempt to avoid responsibility for Doctor Alvord's pronouncements by emphasizing that he as well as John D. Lee was excommunicated from the Mormon Church as soon as his crimes were revealed. Actions speak louder than words, and we have it from Brigham Young's own mouth, 18 years later, in the following statement concerning him: "If anyone comes here and does not conduct himself the way he should, then he will not only find Danites—who are so much spoken of—who will 'bite their horse's heels,' but such wretches will find something that will bite into their own heels as well. In my plain spoken comments I only called things by their rightful names . . ." (Cf. *Deseret News*, Volume 7, 143).[1]

---

1. For a study of the Danites, see Harold Shindler, *Orrin Porter Rockwell: Man of God, Son of Thunder*, 1966. Although a Mormon, Mr. Shindler makes some strong admissions about some of the activities of the Danites. Another book that contains some interesting information on the Danites is Klaus J. Hansen, *Quest For Empire, The Political Kingdom of God and the Council of Fifty in Mormon History* (Lincoln, Neb.: U. of Nebraska, 1974). *Mormonism: Shadow or Reality?* also has an excellent study of the Danites in chap. 28.

11 The Fruits

"By their fruits ye shall know them." Matthew 7:16

[p. 134] In the previous sections I have tried to give a summary presentation of the origin, nature, and development of Mormonism. I should like now to pass on to a consideration of what sort of fruits the system has produced, in order that in that way also we may base a judgment concerning it, even as we recall the words of Him in whose mouth no deceit was found: "A good tree cannot bear evil fruit, and a rotten tree cannot bear good fruit. . . . Therefore ye shall know them by their fruits."[a]

Only the very smallest portion of the crimes of the Mormons have come to light, for who would recount them, after all? The dead do not talk, and murderers seldom are accustomed to bring up the matter of their guilt. Yet even so, we shudder at the number of murders that have been legally attested in Utah. We shudder at them even more because they were committed in the interests of a religious fanaticism and because the laws out there were so trampled under foot that it has not been possible even until

---

a. Matthew 7:18, 20.

now to bring a single one of the murderers to justice.

Undoubtedly most of the crimes were committed in Utah under the so-called reign of terror from 1856 to 1858, before General Johnston's army arrived, while Brigham was carrying out the so-called reformation, in accordance with his [p. 135] insane theories about blood atonement. Judge Cradlebough describes how things were in his judicial district of Southern Utah in the following manner, in a speech which he delivered to a grand jury convened by him in Provo City on March 8, 1859[b]:

> I wish to say to you, gentlemen of the grand jury, that according to what I have discovered, it has been a long time since any judicial authority has been exercised in your district. No one has been punished in the last two years, and yet I have been told that one crime after another has been committed here. . . .

Then the judge drew the special attention of the jury to individual instances like "the Mountain Meadows Massacre," the so-called Springville Murder, and so on, in the hope that in accordance with its oath it might find a well-founded accusation against certain people in connection with specific crimes. In order to guard those who were accused and to protect the witnesses, he additionally requested a detachment of troops from General Johnston. But the Mormon authorities in Provo opposed this and met with Governor Cummings, who protested against military intervention. The result was that the judge had to dismiss the jury after it had been in session for two weeks without finding a true bill, while he himself came to the conclusion that the jury stood under a higher authority than his own—and also that some of the jurymen themselves were accomplices in the crimes involved. In his speech of dismissal Judge Cradlebough said to them:

> I had always believed, until I heard the testimonies in this case (the Springville murder) that I was living in a land with a civil and religious condition such that the Constitution guarantees us the right to travel from one part of the coun-

---

b. The "grand jury" is a kind of secret tribunal which is supposed to find a well-based accusation—"a true bill"—in any criminal process before the offense can be appointed for trial.

try to another, and to worship God according to the conviction of our own conscience. [p. 136] But I am forced to say,
as the testimonies in this case prove, that in regard to Utah,
this assumption has been wrong. People have been murdered there, murdered in a coldblooded and horrible manner. These murders have been deliberated and decided upon
at the council meetings of the Church, and all for this reason, that the victims had fallen away from the Church and
tried to leave the territory. You are mere instruments without a will of your own, the deceived tools of the despotism of
a tyrannical Church. The Leaders of the Church both pay
you and lead you. You are trained to obey their orders and to
commit these gruesome murders. Robbed of your freedom,
you have lost your humanity and have become willing instruments in the hands of evil men.

I tell you, that it will be my most earnest effort, while I am
with you, to break in pieces your religious chains and to set
you free.

As Stenhouse comments in his history, *The Rocky Mountain Saints*,[1] the grand jury would not have tolerated such
language had there not been good reasons for it.

The judge, however, continued to examine these terrible
crimes which were being proved in every detail. But even
left to his own heart, without the assistance of the Governor, he was not able to accomplish anything in this place
where the criminals stood under the protection of the
people themselves. For as he wrote in his court records,
"The whole people stood in organized and united resistance against the enforcement of legal justice."

The circumstances surrounding the Springville murder
are as follows.[2] An old man by the name of Parrish had for
many years belonged to the Mormon Church, but had, like
so many others, become tired of its tyranny. He therefore
decided, since he was wealthy, to move to California with
his family, a wife and two grown sons. This was in the
spring of 1857 during the famous "Reformation." Although

---

1. Stenhouse's book is available through the Utah Lighthouse Ministry in
   Salt Lake City, Utah.
2. *The Valley Tan* carried articles concerning the Springville murders in
   the following issues: March 29, 1859, pp. lff; April 5, 1859, pp. lff; April
   19, 1859, pp. lff; May 17, 1859. *The Valley Tan* is on microfilm at the
   Harold B. Lee Library, BYU. See also Nels Anderson, *Desert Saints—
   The Mormon Frontier in Utah* (Chicago: U. of Chicago Press, 1966).

Parrish to the best of his ability kept his departure a secret
[p. 137] it must still have leaked out, for a certain J. M.
Stewart, who at the time was Bishop Johnson's Adviser,
testifies that at one of their secret Church meetings, a
letter from Brigham Young to the bishop was read aloud.
In it were mentioned certain suspicious people that he
should watch out for, etc. Two men, Durfy and Potter, were
sent as spies to the Parrish family, to win their confidence
by pretending that they too were dissatisfied with Mormonism and desired to leave Utah. The plan succeeded,
and they all agreed to travel to California together. It was
decided to depart by night between the fourteenth and the
fifteenth of March. It was arranged that they should leave
town in two groups. Potter and the old Parrish were to go
first, and then Durfy and the two sons would follow. What
later happened, Durfy relates at a later occasion in court:

Bird was hiding behind a fence corner, and when Parrish
and Potter came walking along the fence, Bird said that he
shot Potter, having taken him to be Parrish. After Bird had
fired, he stood up and walked over to the place where Parrish stood, and Parrish asked him if he was the one who had
shot him. He (Bird) said that Parrish had a gun in his hand
which he then laid down, Bird and Parrish took hold of each
other and Bird, pulling his knife, tried his best to stab Parrish. Bird said that when Parrish had been knocked down,
he (Bird) gave him a slash which slit his throat. He never
said that he had anyone to help him out. Bird said that when
he had finished with the old man, he took Potter's gun and
his own as well, and he went back to the fence corner to be
ready when I and the two young Parrish [men]* would arrive. He said that when we came he fired and saw one man
drop. He said that he feared the one he had hit would run
away, and he therefore shot him again. When Orin Parrish
and I (Durfy) started running, he said that he jumped over
the fence and shot at Orin. He said that he saw me run down
into a ditch, and asked if I had heard him [p. 138] call me. I
answered that I had no desire to, for I didn't know what the
shooting meant! The day after the murder I heard Bishop
Johnson and Bird talking together, and he (the bishop)
scolded Potter and Bird because they had not gone farther
away with them. The bishop said that he wished that I might
be done with the affair, and that I should not even tell him
who it was. If I did so, then they would deal with me in the
same fashion.

*This word
added for
clarity.
—Trans.

This almost led to the consequence that Durfy also was put on the blacklist, even though he was a spy for the Church. The aforementioned counselor of the bishop, J. T. Stewart, relates:

> While the bishop and I were talking together, Bird came in to us and reported in a completely cold-blooded fashion: ". . . When Potter fell, I seized Parrish and killed him with my knife!" I knew that Parrish was killed with a knife. Potter died from four pellets in a single shot which struck him in the left breast, and Beason Parrish was killed by one or two shots into his body.[c]

On the next day the murdered men were brought into the city, and so it became the duty of Counselor Stewart to hold an inquest concerning the murder. In line with the rest of the hypocritical travesties, they had Durfy and Orin Parrish arrested on suspicion of murder; but since neither of them—for very good reason—could furnish any information, they were released again! This is the way that Brigham saves the souls of nonbelievers—by having them killed.

Two or three days before the murder, a carriage and a pair of horses were stolen from Parrish. The widow knew who had taken them, and she appealed to Brigham Young to get them back; but from him she received the advice to just keep quiet about it if she wanted to be well off otherwise. [p. 139] The man who had the horses, a certain Lysander Gee, declared that he had received the horses shortly afterward [and]* that they had been stolen, with orders not to turn them over to anyone else at all. He drove around with the stolen horses gladly enough, while Parrish's widow, who was plunged into poverty and despair, had to live on bread and water. That is the way things go among "the Latter Day Saints of the Church of Jesus Christ."

*This word added for clarity. —Trans.

Bill Hickman, who became so well known all over America and was formerly so generally feared in Utah, and who was along with O. P. Rockwell, the foremost commander of the Danites, has disclosed a great many frightful crimes which he carried out according to the direct

---

c. The quotation here comes from his answer to a question put to him in court.

order and commandment of Brigham Young, according to his own written confession which was published by I. H. Beadle in 1872 in Salt Lake City. Those same crimes, by the way, have also been attested in detail by other people besides Bill Hickman. I will cite only a few instances.

In 1858 while Bill Hickman was away to fight with General Johnston's army (in which conflict he performed duties as captain of an independent corps), he received orders of this sort from Brigham Young (through Joseph A. Young, the oldest son of the prophet) to kill a man named Yates. "This man," says Bill Hickman, "was a kind of merchant who had previously left the mountains but had now come back with a store of goods worth about $6,000," which he had obtained by barter from the Indians. When Johnston went into winter quarters at Fort Bridger, Hickman decided to go home with some of his men in order to recruit horses for themselves and so on. At that same time Yates was taken by one of the Mormons and by the commanding general, D. Wells, and turned over to Hickman with the understanding that "he was supposed to put him to death." As a preliminary to this, Hickman was supposed to take him away to the camp of Colonel Jones, where he presumably would receive further orders. On the way they met J. A. Young, who told them that his father wanted Yates killed, and that Hickman would receive further orders from Colonel Jonas [sic]. By sunset they came to Jones, who took Hickman to one side and said [p. 140] that he had orders to finish Yates off.* Jones and Hickman were agreed about the matter. The murder was committed by the campfire at 12:00 midnight, when no one was present except Jones, Hosea Stout, and another man, who asked if Yates was asleep. Hickman answered, "Yes," and at the same time crushed his head with an axe. A bedcover was thrown over the murdered man, while the others dug a deep hole. Then they buried the corpse and shifted the campfire over the grave so as to hide its location. Hickman and his comrade, Fleck, journeyed down to Salt Lake City and reported at Brigham Young's office. The prophet first asked about the situation in the east and about General Johnston's army, and then afterward about what had become of Yates. Hickman told him. Brigham next wanted to know whether Hickman had received his orders. Hickman answered that he had received instructions both from Jones and from Joseph A. Young. Brigham said that it was

*At this point in the Danish text, Ahmanson cites the literal English phrase used by the speaker, "use him up."—Ed.

certainly a good thing! Hickman then took out $900 in twenty-dollar gold pieces, which were taken from Yates when he was seized, and now they belonged to the prophet. But at the same time he asked to keep a portion of them, because he had had many expenses during the war. The prophet answered that the money had to be spent to defray the costs of the war, and the Danite commander was treated to a scolding for his unreasonable request! "This stinginess," relates Hickman, "removed all the Mormonism from Flack* (his comrade), and he never had a scrap of Mormonism left in him from that time on."

It was for this crime that Bill Hickman was arrested, and according to his indications the grave of the murdered man was discovered and the corpse dug up. Yates's wife, who in 1872 was living in Nevada, had believed the whole time that her husband had been killed by the Indians.

In May 1850 a man named Jesse T. Hartley was murdered, and Hickman recounts as follows:

*Note the author's variation in the spelling of this name even on the same page.
—Trans.

> ... We[d] [p. 141] had climbed over "Big Mountain" and had come three or four miles down to East Canyon, when a Mr. Hartley from Provo City came to meet us and joined our group. This Hartley was a young lawyer who had migrated from Oregon to Salt Lake City the summer before, and had got married to a respectable young woman named Bullock from Provo City. . . . He told me that he had never been accustomed to hard work, and now he was traveling to Fort Bridger or Green River in order to look for a job as a bookkeeper or similar occupation for him to get into. He was a young man with an attractive, intelligent exterior. But at the last April Conference Brigham had given him a terrible character rating and called him all kinds of names and told him he ought to have his throat cut, etc. Hartley declared that he was innocent, but he felt very badly about the whole affair.
>
> I was noticing that Orson Hyde was observing him very closely, and when we had been encamped for an hour or two, Hyde told me that he had had orders from Brigham Young to have Hartley killed, if he got to Fort Supply, the Mormon town in the new settlement. "I want you and George Boyd to do it," he said. Later I saw him and Boyd talking together, whereupon Boyd came over to me and

---

d. Judge Appleby, Orson Hyde, Hickman, and twelve others, who were off on a journey to organize a new county in Utah named Green River.

said, "It's in fine order, Bill; I will help you to kill the fellow."
Two or three wagons were still behind on the trail and Orson
Hyde asked me to ride back and see if there was anything
wrong with them. Boyd saddled his horse to accompany me,
but Hartley came forward and offered to go along, in case
Boyd wanted to have him take his horse. Orson Hyde said,
"Have him take the horse!" and Boyd obeyed. Then Hyde
whispered to me: "Now is the time—don't allow him to
come back!" We went off and after we had ridden about half
a mile we came to a river which rose to half-way up the
sides of our horses. While we were fording across, Hartley
got shot and fell into the river. I kept on riding and I met
Hosea Stout, a Mormon attorney, who told me that the wagons were coming right behind him.

[p. 142] Stout asked me whether I had seen Hartley. I
replied that he had come to our camp. Stout said that according to what he had heard, Hartley was supposed to be
killed. And when I told him what had happened, he said,
"That was good!" Upon my return to camp, Boyd said that
his horse had come to the camp with the saddle smeared
with blood, which he and some other men had washed off in
the brook. Orson Hyde told me that I had done well. He and
some others of the group had climbed the slope of the
mountain and had seen the whole affair from that vantage
point.[e]

Of all of Bill Hickman's cold-blooded murders (each and
every one of which in his confession he had carried out,
according to his constant declaration, in the full belief that
it was his obligation to obey the prophet and the leaders of
the Church) Hartley's murder seems to have weighed the
most heavily upon his conscience. Mr. Beadle, who received the confession, relates that in his conversation with
him, Hickman had tried to avoid this subject—just as his
manuscript at this point was very indistinct, blotted, and
erased, and it testified to an unsure hand and conflicting
emotions.

Fourteen years before Hickman's confession came to
light, a certain Mariette Smith published a book entitled
Fifteen Years Among the Mormons, in which Hartley's murder was also related in detail. From it we should like to
excerpt the following:

Almost a year after this episode (the murder) I saw Jesse
Hartley's widow by Green River, while I was on my way to

e. Cf. Hickman's *Confession.*

the States. She had been a very lovely woman and was even then only twenty-two years old. She appeared to me to be the most grief-stricken, heartsick person I have ever seen. She was living with her brother, who was a Mormon and a ferryman for Green River. While we were waiting to get ferried over, I became aware of this woman with her pale, doleful appearance, [p. 143] sitting alone by the slope of the river in her black mourning clothes.

The two women got acquainted and were sympathizing with each other, when the widow said:

> . . . If you have been married as a Mormon, you must become acquainted with sorrow; but the cruelty I have suffered is certainly beyond compare, even in this pitiless and insensitive country. When I got married to Jesse Hartley, I knew he was not a Mormon, even though he was regarded as such; but this meant nothing to me, for I knew that he was a noble-minded man who sought only that which was right. Our wedding brought him into close contact with the leading men of the Church. In this way he came to know something that he could scarcely believe, and which would damage us if it got out among the "heathen." I was completely unaware of these things, although I had been brought up among the "Saints."
>
> I don't understand all that he uncovered, nor in general what he was doing. But they found out that he had written against the Church, and for that reason he was excommuni-

---

f. On Sunday, September 21, 1856, this doctrine of blood atonement was publicly preached by Brigham Young and his second adviser, A. M. Grant, to the Saints in the Tabernacle in the following fashion: "There are sins," the prophet says, "which are committed and which cannot be forgiven either in this world or in the world to come. And if the sinner had his eyes open so that he could see his true condition, then he would be perfectly willing to let his blood be shed upon earth as an atoning sacrifice for his sins. But if that does not take place, then his sins cleave closely to him and follow after him in the world to come. . . . I will say further that there are men who have come to me in order to offer up their lives as an atonement for their sins. . . . There are sins which can be atoned for by a sacrifice on the altar just as in ancient times; and there are sins which the blood of a lamb, a calf or a turtledove cannot atone for, but which must be expiated by the sinner's own blood. This is the reason why men speak to you from this place (i.e., the Tabernacle pulpit) as they do. They understand this doctrine and let a few words fall concerning it." "Brothers and sisters," says I. M. Grant, "we want you to turn yourselves around and forsake your sins. And you who have committed sins which cannot be effaced by baptism (baptism is repeated after any crime in the case of the Mormons—author's comment) let your blood be poured out, and let some of it rise up as an atonement offering for your sins." So reproduced in the organ of the Church, *Deseret News*, October 1, 1859.

cated, and Brigham wanted him to give up his life as an atonement for his sins[f] that he should allow himself to be sacrificed in the Endowment House, where such atonements take place. I knew nothing about this until my husband told me about it. But it is true, they kill those who have committed such great sins that they cannot be atoned for in any other way. The prophet says that if they submit themselves to this, he can save them; otherwise they are lost. [p. 144] Oh it is terrible, but my husband did not want to let himself be sacrificed, and therefore he was going off to the United States alone, in the hope that he might achieve possible success there. I told him when he left me that he would be killed, and so he was. Bill Hickman and another Danite shot him at the mountain pass, and I have often been compelled to wait on Hickman when he passes this way, even though I knew the whole time that he was the one who was my husband's murderer. My child soon followed his father, and I hope that I also will soon follow them, too. Why should I keep on living? They have brought me here, and I would rather live here than go back to Salt Lake, where my husband's murderers put a curse upon the ground they walk on and live on unpunished in their lusts!

It stands written: "God does not wish the death of the sinner, but that he should turn back and live." Is this perchance the sentence that Brigham Young lays down as a basis for his teaching about the blood atonement? Furthermore: "God so loved the world, that He gave up His only Son, that whoever believes in Him shall not be lost but have eternal life." The first message at Christ's birth was: "Peace on earth and good will among men!" His name was to be Prince of Peace, and He came to "shine unto those who sit in darkness and in the shadow of death . . . in order to guide our feet in the way of peace."

[p. 145] Again, it is written: "Everyone who does evil hates the light and does not come to the light lest his deeds should convict him." The Mormons' deadly hatred toward all that they call "apostate" is principally based on the fear that their evil, abominable deeds may through them be brought to light. To furnish an example of the impudence and the crudity with which the Mormon prophets express themselves on such occasions, we quote a few statements by Brigham Young concerning a man named Gladen Bishop, who along with several others of the so-called Gladenites was unwilling to recognize Brigham Young* as the successor of the murdered Prophet:

*These words added for clarity. The original Danish reads "B.Y."—Ed.

. . . Shut your mouths! (Brigham said to them) or else a speedy destruction will overtake you" (cf. Journal of Discourses, Volume 1, page 62) I will draw out my knife (i.e., Bowie knife) and either conquer or die. . . . A man like that should be sliced in two just below the ears. . . . I would like to take my "breast-pin" I used to wear in Nauvoo, and slice his . . . throat in two from the one ear to the other and say: "Go straight to hell!"*

Heber C. Kimball says with brutal cynicism of heart and a loathsome mask of hypocrisy: "Truly I pray for my enemies! I pray to Almighty God to damn them!" Presumably no comments are needed about statements like these!

"Of all the cowardly and gruesome deeds that the Mormon priesthood ever performed in an abominable and hateful manner, the first place is taken by the murder of the Aikens Party," says the aforementioned Mr. Beadle.

The Mountain Meadows Massacre exceeds it in magnitude, to be sure, but not in wanton cruelty, treachery, and violation of hospitality, which is regarded as sacred even among the Indians and other savage races. For fourteen years the blood of the murdered victims had cried out from the ground before the truth came to light. But now that the authority of the national government has been established in Utah, witnesses are coming forward in droves, and every detail of this terrible tragedy has been proved.*

[p. 146] From the statements of the witnesses who came before the grand jury and are now in the hand of the appropriate officials, I have put together the following account of the murder perpetrated on the Aikens group. It consisted of six men: John Aiken, William Aiken, Busch, a man called "the Colonel," and two others whose names the witnesses do not remember. One of them was a smith, another was a cabinetmaker, and two tradesmen. It is not known what occupations the other two had. They left Sacramento early in May 1857, and they were traveling eastward to meet General Johnston's army. When they got to the Humboldt River, they found that the Indians were very hostile, and so they decided to wait there for a larger Mormon group, which at that time had received orders to return home from their settlements in Carson Valley. In company with the Mormons they then continued their journey to Salt Lake. John Pendleton, one of the Mormons,

*At this point in the Danish text, Ahmanson cites the literal English phrase used by the speaker, "go to hell cross lots."—Ed.

*At this point, a printing or editing error in the original text omits the closing quotation marks that indicate where Beadle's remarks end and Ahmanson's commentary resumes. We end Beadle's remarks here arbitrarily. —Ed.

says in his statement about them, "A finer group of men I have never seen. They were courteous, good-hearted, honest, and always ready to carry out every task needful upon the way."

The Mormon's wagon train was making only slow progress, and so the Aikens party left them behind when they were about 100 miles distant from Salt Lake City, and were proceeding on. But upon their arrival at Kanesville twenty-five miles north of Salt Lake, they were all arrested on the pretext that they were spies for the US government. A few days later Pendleton and the Mormons arrived there, and they found Aiken's horses in the corral of the church. When it was asked what the reason was for that, they were informed that Aiken had been arrested for espionage. "Spies?" answered Pendleton, ". . . They traveled the whole way with us, and they didn't know the least thing about the army." "We don't care anything about that; we are holding them anyhow!" answered the man who was in charge of the corral. Aiken and his comrades had property and money with them to the amount of $25,000. They were taken into the town and kept under arrest in a house at the corner of Main Street and First South-Fourth Street. But since no evidence could be found against them, it was indicated to them that they were going to be sent out [p. 147] of the Territory by the southern route. So four of them proceeded on their way, but Buck and one of the other men remained behind in the town. The ones who were traveling were escorted by O. P. Rockwell, John Lot, Miles, and a fourth man. When they reached Nephi, which lies 100 miles south of Salt Lake, Rockwell notified Bryant, the bishop of the town, that he had orders to finish these men off. Then Bishop Bryant convened a council right away, and the following men were chosen to help out: I. Bigler (now a bishop), P. Pitchforth (Bryant's chief advisor), John Kinck, and Pickton.

The doomed men lodged with the T. B. Footes and (strangely enough) some member of that family testified that they had heard the actions taken by the council when the sentence of death was decided upon. But the murderers stole out of the tithe-house at 11:00 P.M. in order to set themselves in ambush for Aiken's party, who set out on their way at dawn. When they reached the Sevier River, Porter Rockwell told them that they had to stop there, since they would not find any suitable campsite for the following day. Soon after they had set up camp, the murderers came up and asked for permission that they might stay there also, and this was granted. The tired men now divested themselves of their weapons, their heavy outer garments, etc., and soon afterwards had fallen into a deep sleep, from which neither of them were ever to awaken in this life. Everything was set for carrying out the satanic plan and yet a seeming apprehension deterred them. From what was confessed, they seem to have been afraid that the murder could not be carried out in full secrecy, and so they decided not to use their firearms. On this account Porter Rockwell's men and the bishop's people from Hephi attacked the sleeping men with stakes and iron bolts which they got from the wagons. Two of them died without making any movement, but John Aiken jumped up only slightly wounded and ran off into the bushes, where a shot fired by John Kink [sic] knocked him unconscious to the ground. The colonel also made it to the bushes after receiving a musket ball in one shoulder from Rockwell's rifle; and because he thought that the attack was coming from a band of robbers, he got back to Nephi as quickly [p. 148] as possible. By an almost supernatural effort he covered the twenty-five miles and reached Nephi just as the first rays of the sun burst over the eastern cliffs of Utah. That young, strong, handsome man who had left Nephi the morning of the previous day, now stumbled his way, pale as death, weak and bleeding through the streets of the city to the house of Bishop Foote, where his report evoked a well-feigned horror.

Meanwhile the gang of murderers had gathered up the other three and cast them into the river on the supposition that they were dead. But John Aiken regained consciousness and crawled to the shore on the same side and then hid himself in the brush, where he overheard the following conversations: "Are all the accursed heathen dead, Rockwell?" "Yeah, all except one, who ran away—that devil!" Aiken, who assumed that he was the one they were talking about, kept on lying very still until the Danites had gone off. Then he proceeded on the way to Nephi in the cold of night, while the ground was covered with snow, without hat, coat, or boots. Who can imagine how the man felt? He was no longer unaware, as the "Colonel" was, of who the murderers were, and he assumed that he was the only survivor. He knew that there was little hope of deliverance in Nephi, but that was the only place available. The next day, when he reached Nephi after incredible effort, he fell down exhausted in front of the first door he got to. Yet it seemed that the first words that he heard instilled new life into him, for the woman of the house, who later became a witness in the case, exclaimed: "Look, here is another one who has also escaped from the robbers! One is already at the house of Brother Foote."—"God be praised! It is my brother," exclaimed Aiken, and he continued his way to that house. The people of the town were appalled as they related how he looked at that time. His hair was smeared with dried blood and all his movements were like those of a drunken man. Instead of his brother it was "the Colonel" whom he met at Foote's. They fell into each other's bleeding arms with a convulsive sobbing and kissing to testify to their feelings and emotional state. Even a demon would have to have felt compassion at such [p. 149] a sight, but the Mormons felt none at all. A tiger can be enticed away from his victim, a bear can be tamed, and a hyena can be weaned from a thirst for blood, but only religious fanaticism can overcome all feelings of pity or sympathy and make a man into a monster that can only be found like those of the nethermost regions, where devils alone hold sway. While this moving scene was going on, these demons took counsel together once more, and decided upon the death of the two escapees. Bishop Bryant came in and advised them to get back to Salt Lake as quickly as possible, after he had first extracted the bullets and bandaged their wounds. One of Bishop Foote's sons appeared to befriend them, and Aiken asked him to write down a description of the entire episode. Aiken himelf had begun to put it in writing, but he felt so overwhelmed that he asked young Foote to do it for him. The description was written out, and the dying statements of Aiken and the "Colonel" are still extant.

After the return of the murderers new plans were laid. Aikens [sic] had saved a pistol and the "Colonel" a gold watch that was worth $250. When they were about to leave the town and asked how much they owed, the reply was, "Thirty dollars!" They promised to send this sum from Salt Lake, but they soon came to see that they would not be allowed to get off in this manner. Then Aikin [*sic*] answered: "Here is my revolver and my comrade's watch; take what you have a mind to!" After Aiken gave it to Foote, he said: "There, take my best friend—but God knows it will be of little use to us!"—Thereupon he turned to his companion and said with tears in his eyes: "Prepare yourself for death, Colonel, for we shall never get out of this valley alive." According to the Nephi woman previously mentioned, who was one of the principal witnesses in the case, these men were regarded by everyone as doomed to death. They had come five miles out of Nephi when their coachman, a Mormon named Woolie, halted the carriage near an old house, unharnessed the horses and led them off on the pretext of watering them. Thereupon two men came out of the house with double-barreled muskets which they fired at them. Aiken and the Colonel were both shot through the head [p. 150] and fell down from the carriage to the ground. The corpses were weighted down with stones and let down into one of the "bottomless" springs of which many are to be found in that place.

"I was passing by this place," said Mr. Beadle, "in 1869 and at that time I heard a report told by the local inhabitants of how some bad men had been plunged into that spring. . . ." Meanwhile Rockwell and his gang arrived at Salt Lake City and brought with them the two remaining men (Buck and one of the unknown persons) down south after having got them drunk with brandy. Yet it is possible that Buck was just playing the part of a drunk; but the other man was altogether unconscious by the time they reached the mountain pass where they were to be finished off. They were assulted with cudgels and deadly lead-shot slings, and the unknown fellow was killed instantly, whereas Buck jumped out of the carriage and ran away, although his pursuers fired three shots after him. Buck swam across the Jordan River and followed its left bank so as to arrive at Salt Lake City. There his accounts of what had happened soon caused a great deal of unpleasant common talk. . . . Bill Hickman was then brought in so that he might "finish off the business," and the way in which he carried this out he explains himself in his own confessions:

> . . . I immediately took to horse and rode over to Brigham Young's office. He asked me "whether I had the boys." I

asked, "Which boys?" He answered, "George Grant and William Kimball." I told him that I had received orders to meet
them at his office, whereupon he answered, "The boys have
done some bungling; they were all of them drunk. They
wounded a guy and let him run away from them by the
mountain peaks. Now he has come to town and his stories
are making a bad stink." He ordered me to finish him off
(i.e. Buck) and "destroy him."

Since a man named Dalton who lived twelve miles north
of Salt Lake City, on whose property Aiken's party had
stayed for some weeks, just (happened)* to be in town,
therefore Grant and Kimball arranged things in such a
way that Dalton should invite Buck to come home with
him. Hickman obtained a description of Dalton's horse,
and so on, and he went on ahead of them in company
[p. 151] with one of "the boys" named Meachum. "We
proceeded on our way," said Hickman,

*This word
added for
clarity.
—Trans.*

> to the spot which had been chose, and just then in the
> darkness along came Dalton driving. We cried, "Halt!" and
> Buck received a shot through his head and fell over the
> railing down into a ditch. A cloth was hung up on one of the
> bushes in order to indicate the spot. We rode back to town
> and at General Grant's, whose home had been determined as
> our rendezvous, we found Kimball, O. P. Rockwell, and
> some others. They asked if everything went O.K. I answered,
> "Yes, it did." Then they brought shovels along and we all
> went back to the place, dug the pit deeper and buried him
> in it. Then we went back to Grant's, were treated with bran-
> dy and then we bid one another good night.[g]

Fourteen years afterward, in 1872, Brigham Young, Bill
Hickman, General Wells, and O. P. Rockwell were arrested
for complicity in this murder.[3] This time the case at least
was taken to court, but on the basis of some virtually
inconsequential defect in procedural matters, all those
murderers were released, and Salt Lake City's citizens had
the pleasure of seeing the Danite commander upon the
city streets, swinging his hat and crying "Hurrah!" in hon-
or of American law and order.

---

g. Cf. *Hickman's Confession.*

3. See *Mormonism: Shadow or Reality?* pp. 554ff.

12 The Mountain Meadows Massacre

[p. 152] In the middle of September 1857 a company of emigrants from Arkansas, consisting of about 120 men, women, and children, were murdered in Mountain Meadows, Washington County, Utah Territory.[1] People who were traveling between California and Utah saw the dead bodies lying around in the meadow and gave a shuddering report of it. In Utah they replied that Indians had done it, and this account was accepted for some time. But such a frightful mystery could not remain hidden for very long. A rumor was spread that it was the Mormons who had perpetrated the massacre at the instigation of Brigham Young! And this of course gave the affair a considerably increased and sinister interest. Without doubt the Mountain Meadows massacre forms one of the blackest chapters in the dark history of Mormonism. We should now endeavor to give a vivid but succinct presentation of this deed of treachery in the order of the successive scenes which have thus far come to light.

---

1. For a thorough study of the Mountain Meadows Massacre see Juanita Brooks, *Mountain Meadows Massacre* (Norman, Okla.: U. of Oklahoma Press, 1964).

Excerpt of an Open Letter from "Argus" to Brigham Young.[a]

Sir:

The company of emigrants who were murdered at Mountain Meadows in your jurisdiction on the fifteenth [p. 153] of September 1857, was one of the most well-to-do, peaceable and respectable groups that ever traveled across the continent by way of Salt Lake City! Those authentically American citizens in United States territory at that time set up their tents by the Jordan River, an open, unsold, unfenced public domain. And according to Utah's laws their cattle and possessions were likewise inviolable in that location. The majority of these emigrants were fellow countrymen of a plain and simple life-style; and since you never accused them of thievery, robbery, encroachment, or disturbance of public order, or for unseemly conduct in general, then it is only reasonable that these people were as honest in their attitudes, and likewise as honorable and upright in their contacts with others, as the people of the land generally are. As they encamped by the Jordan, tired and worn out, their store of provisions was virtually used up, and their draught animals were almost unusable after the long, difficult journey. It was necessary for them to remain in Utah until they had obtained a new stock of provisions and their exhausted draught animals had been replaced with new ones, and they themselves had regained renewed strength. Utah had just had an abundant harvest that year; the hills and valleys were covered with richly nourishing grass. What was there to hinder the emigrants from staying there as long as they pleased? Why couldn't they buy whatever they needed and then continue their journey whenever they pleased? Of what offense were they guilty, that the law, which was represented by your person, did not have to protect them? Why were they ordered to break camp and travel on? Or even worse—why was a courier sent out with a written mandate to all Mormons along the travel route of the emigrants not to have the least contact [p. 154] with these poor people in the matter of trade or dealings [of any kind]?* For that was almost tantamount to consigning them to inescapable starvation in the wilderness!

*These words added for clarity.—Trans.

You were at that time the Governor of Utah, the Commander-in-chief of the Militia and Superintendent for Indian Affairs, and therefore also a sworn official of the United

---

a. The "Open Letter" under the pseudonymn of "Argus" first appeared as an article in a "Gentile" newspaper called the *Corinne Reporter*, which earlier appeared in Utah, and aroused a great sensation.

States and of the Territory. The preservation of the most sacred liberties and rights of the people was entrusted to you. It was incumbent upon you as an important and serious obligation to extend to all the protection of the law within the boundaries of your authority, without regard to religion, name, nationality or personal feelings. You were also the high priest of almost the entire people and you presented yourself as possessing extraordinary supernatural authority as well as being an especially exceptional adviser from heaven. To put it plainly, you claimed to be the representative of our heavenly Redeemer upon earth, the exponent of the great Teacher of love and lovingkindness, His follower whose final words were: "Father, forgive them. . . !

Since the emigrants were not allowed to stay by the Jordan, they broke camp and continued their journey in the direction of Los Angeles, but they could of course make only slow progress.

Upon arrival at "American Fort Settlement" they tried to buy provisions and exchange some of their worn-out beasts for fresh, strong Mormon animals. Yet however advantageous terms they offered, none of the parties contacted—much to their surprise—allowed any transaction at all. Not the least significant item could be purchased, from them, even though meal, meat, vegetables, poultry, butter, eggs, etc. were abundantly available. Then they traveled on through Battle Creek, Provo, Springville, Spanish Fork, Payson, Salt Creek, Fillmore, trying in every place to buy provisions and trade cattle, but everywhere in vain. It is true that one or two hardy Mormons occasionally slipped into the emigrants' camp at night—thereby exposing themselves to incurring punishment marked out as "reward for disobedience to orders," but such small trifles naturally contributed but [p. 155] little for such a large company. . . . Despite the provoking treatment they received in this fashion, the emigrants conducted themselves toward the Mormons in a friendly and peaceable manner. No complaints or accusations were directed against them, and it was obviously their purpose to pass through Utah in order to reach if possible a Gentile (i.e., a non-Mormon) settlement, where they could buy themselves something to eat by means of their money and cattle. As it was well known, a lot of emigrant trains from the eastern states on their way to California were accustomed to get provisioned for their journey as far as Salt Lake City. There they would get supplied once more for the trip to California. This has happened innumerable times without the least difficulty on the part of the Mormons. What was it that led to such an unusual and unprovoked mode of procedure toward these particular emigrants? Why couldn't they obtain provisions and rest up, the way all the others did? Because they were from Arkansas! That is, from the state in which your fellow "apostle," Parley P. Pratt, had recently been killed. . . !

We left the unfortunate emigrants in Fillmore, people who were undertaking a trip with empty wagons and worn-out draught animals across America's most fearful wilderness. The next town they passed through was Corn Creek, and here they met the first friendly glance and heard the first loving words since they left the Jordan. And how strange! It was Indians who lived there! These savages sold them thirty bushels of maize, all that they could do without, and they allowed them to depart in peace! But by that time the emigrants had passed through fifteen settlements inhabited by "Latter Day Saints of Jesus Christ" who refused to sell them any food!

In truth this was a significant kind of application of the words, "If thine enemy hunger, then give him food. . . ." From Corn Creek the travelers came to Beaver and found the usual noncooperation on the part of the Mormons. They then went on to Parowan, but there they were not permitted even to enter the town, even though the Federal Government had paid out $25,000 in gold for the construction of the highway which the emigrants had followed the whole time from Salt Lake City, and which led directly through [p. 156] the town of Parowan! They were compelled to leave the public highway and detour around the west side of the town. They set up camp by a small stream near the town, and attempted to buy cattle and provisions, but all in vain. Then they asked if they might get their maize ground at the corn mill in Parowan, that is, the maize that they had bought from the Indians at Corn Creek, but this also was denied them. A little Englishman wanted to go out to sell them a few provisions, but Bishop Lewis's son and councilor compelled him with a drawn Bowie knife to go back and give up his kindhearted purpose!

Dear sir! Why was it forbidden to these emigrants to travel through or to enter Parowan? Perhaps this question will be put to you some day by the kind of authority that will find you constrained to give an answer, no matter how unpleasant for you it may be! You can answer it, along with your adjutant and brigadier general, George M. Smith, and William H. Dame as well, the colonel of a military company under your command, colonel of the regiment, who a short while later attacked the defenseless emigrants at Mountain Meadows and murdered them! But you do not answer until you are compelled to! Let me then assume that Parowan was the headquarters of this regiment, that it was Colonel Dame's residence, that there were certain military installations within the ramparts which it would not be wise for the emigrants to have any suspicion of. For their destruction was to be carried out by means of a surprise attack, so that the consequence should be prevented that the peaceable nature and fine behavior of the emigrants might find some kind of sympathy in Parowan if they came into direct contact. For the Mormons' passive hostility was now very shortly to become activistic!

From there the emigrants arrived at Cedar City, which at that time had the most inhabitants of all the towns of southern Utah. Here they were allowed to purchase fifty bushels of tithe-wheat, and also to get this wheat and the maize ground in John D. Lee's mill. Yet this favor was scarcely worthy of thanks, for the authorities who sold the corn were definitely counting on getting it back again within a week. In any [p. 157] case the emigrants were thereby only half provisioned for their journey to the nearest inhabited location, San Bernardino in California—as all experienced men who have traveled by this route can verify.

After a day's stopover in Cedar City the people from Arkansas continued their journey, the tragic conclusion of which was near at hand. It took them three days to travel the twenty miles between Cedar City and Iron Creek. Beyond that two days were spent in journeying from Iron Creek to Mountain Meadows, a distance of about fifteen miles. These facts speak eloquently of their pitiable, worn-out condition.

In the meantime a war council [was]* held in Parowan, and [was]* attended by president Isaac C. Haight (the Mormon high priest in southern Utah), Colonel Dame, Major J. D. Lee and their adjutant. They issued a mobilization order to the "Nauvoo legion" to assemble "armed and equipped as the law prescribes in case of war." The regiment was organized in Cedar City under the command of its Major Jon D. Lei [sic] and it started off from there—escorted by the baggage carts and the customary military supplies, except for artillery—and went in pursuit of the emigrants on the same day that they left Iron Creek. Lee, who was also the Indian Agent for Southern Utah, invited the Piute Indians to guide him, and in this way he controlled a force of troops which the unfortunate emigrants could not hope to withstand.

*This word added for clarity.
—Ed.

*This word added for clarity.
—Ed.

The intention had actually been to assail the emigrants at Clara Crossing, but they were not overtaken until the morning of September twelfth by Mountain Meadows, just at the moment when these people, who had no inkling of the slightest danger, were beginning their day's journey. No sooner had they gone a fair distance on their way from the spring by which they had camped overnight, than the Indians without Lee's knowledge began to fire at them. Naturally the emigrants were very greatly surprised, but they did not immediately lose their wits, for they had for a long time been traveling through unsafe Indian territory. Within a few minutes they stood prepared for a brave response from behind [p. 158] a barricade of wagons, but alas, they were cut off from the water!

For two days they nevertheless held out so bravely against the troops that Lee began to get uneasy. He therefore sent messengers to Washington and to Cedar City for reinforcements. These were speedily called up and marched off and joined up with Lee on the morning of the fourth day after the attack. This last conscription included all the fighting men in Washington, and only twenty remained behind in Cedar City. The third day of the battle the emigrants could no longer do without water. The most terrible thirst almost deprived them of their wits. They could see the water, but the gunfire from the Mormon rifles prevented them from access to it. Various ones lost their lives in an unsuccessful, desperate attempt to reach it. At last as they were dying of thirst they dressed two little girls in white and let them run down toward the spring with a bucket, in the hope that the Mormons might retain just a trace of humanity. But the Mormons shot the little ones dead!

The day after the reinforcements arrived, Lee called his troops together at the break of dawn just about half a mile from the emigrants' defense line and he delivered a speech in which he informed them that he had received orders from "headquarters" to kill all of the emigrant company except for the children! You, sir, unless I am mistaken, will have to come into agreement some day with Colonel Dame as to whether those "headquarters" were in Salt Lake City or in Parowan; and I should be very surprised if the Colonel will accept in court the responsibility for himself alone in regard to those extraordinary orders. But however this may turn out, there can be no doubt that such orders were actually issued.

Two councils of war were held in Parowan. The first was at about the same time as the emigrants were passing around the city. Haight and Lee were present both times, but when the last war council was over, they both rode back together to Cedar City. Lee went off to take command of [p. 159] the troops, and Haight went to get ready for furnishing him with assistance if necessary. It was testified under oath that Haight, two days after the emigrants had left Cedar City, told certain people there (whose names I will not mention right now) that he had received orders from headquarters "to kill all of the emigrants except the small children." This statement must make it obvious to everyone that both Haight and Lee were acting in conformity to a command from higher levels. The idea that Colonel Dame issued this order originally is quite absurd and altogether unlikely, for the colonel of a regiment has no right to undertake anything under such circumstances unless he is thereby carrying out the commands of his superiors. He would be court-martialed if he assumed such authority on his own; but there is certainly no one who has heard any mention of Colonel Dame or Major Lee being hailed before a court-martial on account of their military exploits at Mountain Meadows!

After John D. Lee had informed his soldiers of the fateful order and had instructed them about how they should carry out the whole maneuver, he then went over to the emigrants under a flag of truce and offered to protect them if they would lay down their arms! This offer did not come from sly, untrustworthy Indians, but from Major Lee, a Christian and an officer of the government! What were the emigrants to do? They had not been vanquished, to be sure, but they were under great strain, worn down and half dying of thirst! They accepted the offer, abandoned their small defense line, laid down their weapons, and went over to Lee, who was standing close by the spring, and they placed themselves under his protection! And now a scene took place the horror of which is scarcely to be imagined—even though the description of it may be adequate to fill the heart of any man with revulsion and abhorrence.

Major Lee took these half swooning, unarmed and defenseless men under his protection! That is, he immediately stationed all the men in a single line, and had the women and children go on ahead. Then he began to have them [p. 160] march about half a mile in the direction of Cedar City. From the head of the column he then gave them orders to halt, and immediately afterward he issued the command, "Shoot them down!" along the ranks (of his soldiers). The first salvo was fired before the wretched emigrants understood the situation. Those who were still alive then uttered a heartrending shriek and started fleeing in every direction. But this only started a chase after the men which in its unbounded barbarity may long remain unequaled. . . . Soon everything became quiet and calm except for a hoarse death-rattle here or there, doleful cries from the surviving infants, and perhaps some deep, heavy breathing from the pale, shuddering soldiers who were now surveying the bloody scene in front and all about them.

Although the horrible massacre had now been carried out in this fashion, yet the final end of the horrors had not yet arrived. No! Some of the Mormon soldiers now began to engage in something that seemed even more revolting. They plundered the dead bodies of their victims. The bodies of the younger and older men, of respectable women and chaste young mothers were left lying around without burial, after they had first with bestial merriment been robbed of all their clothing! . . . . The emigrants' wagons, livestock and the rest of their possessions were of course also regarded as fine prizes of war. This was all taken to Cedar City and sold there, partially, at least, under the clever label: "Articles taken at the siege of Sebstopol."

. . . The orders, to be sure, read that the small children should be spared, yet various ones of them perished on the moor of slaughter. Only seventeen were saved, and these were taken under the care of Bishop Klingon Smith. Lee had assigned this responsibility to him before the massacre, but John Willis and Samuel Mardy voluntarily assisted him in this. The hapless orphans were set in the baggage carts of the regiment and then driven off by way of Hamlin's Ranch to Cedar City, where they were distributed among various Mormon families. . . . Later on one or two of these children made some comments about the massacre that were regarded as dangerous; but then they were taken away. . . and they were buried! . . .

[p. 161] Such was the account in the "Argus." Several eyewitnesses relate the following gruesome details about the massacre. After the first salvo was fired at the emigrants, a young girl ran up to the son of Major Lee and entreated his protection. A humane impulse was aroused in the young man's breast at the sight of the pretty little girl clinging to him to save her life, and he decided to save her. But immediately his father came running up and forced his son aside by grabbing him around the neck, and he shot the girl in the face with his revolver, so that she fell lifeless at his feet. Young Lee is said to have been very sorrowful and melancholy [over this]* from that time on.

We shall be speaking later on about the prosecution of Lee in July 1875, but at this point we insert two of the statements of witnesses that came out during that trial, in order to bring into perspective the picture [there presented]* of the Mountain Meadows Massacre.

Robert Keyes stated,

> In 1857 I was traveling from California to Utah. I arrived at the first location in October. At that time I passed through Mountain Meadows southwest of Cedar City. I saw two piles of corpses there. One consisted of women and children, the other of men. The corpses were completely naked and seemed to be thrown carelessly together. They looked as if they had been murdered. I think there were sixty or seventy corpses of women and children. I saw [just]* one man in the pile. The children ranged from one month to twelve years in age. The small kids had been for the most part eaten up by wolves and crows. The necks of some of them had been cut open, others had stab wounds, while still others were riddled with musketballs. All of the corpses were more or less decomposed, except for one corpse of a woman who was lying a little to the southwest of the heap and had a bullet in her left side just below the heart. This corpse showed no sign of putrefacation and was untouched by the wild animals. The expression on her face was peaceful, she seemed to be asleep. The murder had been recently committed. The bodies had apparently been lying there for only fifteen or sixteen days. I passed by there on the Second of October. There were eleven in our group, and seven of them came over to view the murdered men who were lying around in the vicinity. I didn't go. The bodies were naked, so far as I could see, except for a stocking which was on the leg of [p. 162] one of them.

The other witness, Asahel Bennett, declared:

> I was at Mountain Meadows in 1857 about two months after the massacre. I came driving by in December and I saw a bunch of skeletons, among which were skulls of women and children with long, drooping hair all smeared with dried blood. I took note of a child's skeleton, and I also saw skeletons of women, but I didn't know how many of them they were. The bones appeared to have been thrown into some holes or ditches, and they were covered over with earth. But

*These words added for clarity.
—Trans.

*These words added for clarity.
—Trans.

*This word added for clarity.
—Trans.

the wolves had dug them up and scattered them around. I felt deeply moved at this sight, and I remained there only two or three minutes, which seemed to be about so many hours. The spot is located about thirty miles southwest of Cedar City.

In the year 1859 Major Carlton on a trip from California to Utah passed by the spot with a company of U.S. Cavalry. The bleached bones of the emigrants were still lying there, but the officer had them gathered together and built up a large heap of stones with a tall cross on top of them. On one of the stones was carved the following inscription: "Here lie the bones of 120 men, women and children who were murdered on the sixteenth of September, 1857." On the cross-bar of the cross was written: "Vengeance is mine, saith the Lord, and I will requite it."

The monument is said to have been destroyed the first time Brigham Young visited the spot. A man who happened to be present relates: "Brigham said to his followers that the inscription should have read: 'Vengeance is Mine, saith the Lord, and I have requited it!' "

Naturally it seems like a fabulous tale that such a massacre could have taken place in any civilized state in our times. But in the first place, one cannot without qualification call Utah a civilized state. For civilization in part, at least, pertains to the exalted teachings of Christianity concerning love for one's neighbor and equal rights for all men, and basic foundations of government, and a people's sentiments about right and wrong. A vengeance such as the secret endowment of Mormonism prescribes [p. 163] (cf. that section in this book) with the conquest of countries and states and with the subjugation and destruction of their inhabitants—these are principles belonging to a long-vanished era of the history of the human race and still discoverable only among such races as the strangler sects of India, which remain outside the orbit of civilization. The true teachings of Christianity and the enlightenment of our times can no longer combine such absurd notions with the characteristics and attributes of divine origin. Yet this frightful story of the Mountain Meadows Massacre and several others like it which we have here described, and which now will always adhere to the name of this people—these testify to the possibility of the sudden reversion [to barbarism]* on the part of a people from Christianity

*These words added for clarity.—Trans.

and the lofty concepts of true civilization. After almost 1900 years, the divine, philanthropic teachings of Christ have still only partially succeeded in making an impression on a small portion of the human race. But it has taken barely half of one generation for the leaders of Mormonism to sink the symbol of the cross to a lower status than that of the Islam crescent!

Although it may appear incredible to many, it is nevertheless true that Mormonism, like the teachings of Brahma or of Islam, is actually a new religion and has as little in common with Christianity as they do. Mormonism does not believe in "one God" like Mohammed, nor in a "Trinity" as the Christians do; but it believes in many gods, and so they are polytheists to just as great an extent as they are polygamists.

The basic idea in Mormonism, therefore, was from the very beginning that there should be a new state, a new and powerful kingdom on earth (which Daniel and the prophets, of course, predicted), which would now emerge to conquer and hold sway over the earth. With such lofty and fanatical ideas it was of course unthinkable that Mormons would for very long tolerate or be subject to persecution, and it was not long before they became armed. It was still a hopeless matter to carry on open warfare with their enemies ("the heathen"), and so they tried, as we have said, to avenge themselves in a different way. Their expulsion from Missouri and Illinois, [p. 164] the murder of their Prophet, among other things, they have with terrible oaths and covenants sworn to avenge, and Brigham Young has never allowed this duty to be set aside. In addition to this it happened that the oldest and most respected apostle, Parley P. Pratt,[b] was killed in the summer of 1857 in the State of Arkansas, without his murderer being punished by the appropriate authorities.

---

b. Pratt was murdered in Arkansas in 1857 by Mr. McLean, with whose wife he had been married for a considerable time. He had now made plans to abduct the children also of her former husband. These children were being fostered by their grandparents, who lived in Louisiana. She made her way to them, pretending remorse and repentance. She was believed by them and forgiven and she soon won over the trust of her children. After she had got them converted to Mormonism, she moved to Arkansas, where Pratt was waiting to meet them, and it was there that the embittered father caught up to them and shot the apostle. Mrs. McLean was Pratt's third wife.

*This word
added for
clarity.
—Trans.

This episode in conjunction with the circumstance that the new governor was on his way to Utah with the [other]* officials, conducted by the US troops, in order to impose the law and authority of the Union, by force of arms if necessary, served to inflame Mormon fanaticism anew and the exacting of a terrible degree of vengeance as well— especially since Brigham Young had decided to remain the governor and despot of Utah himself. A standing army was set up and the Territory was put on a war footing. It was under these circumstances that the luckless emigrants from Arkansas were passing through Utah. Undoubtedly we can to a large extent ascribe to the above-mentioned circumstances the immediate occasion for the terrible Mountain Meadows massacre. But though these circumstances partially explain the reason, the deed itself naturally continues to be revolting in the highest degree. Indignation over it was sustained through the fact that individual participants in the massacre who had been coerced were undoubtedly pricked in conscience and contributed sworn statements to the court concerning it. The press many times raised a clamor for instituting a court action against the chief [p. 165] figures involved in the crime—or "the dogs of Mountain Meadows," as their neighbors appropriately called them. Yet that did not take place until after the United States took over possession of the Territory, and that unfortunately with a very unsatisfactory result.

On March 8, 1859, fifty-seven of the most important participants (among whom were Isaac C. Haight, John M. Highbee, John D. Lee, William Slade, John Willies, Ira Allen, Joel White) were arraigned before the grand jury in Provo City. The district judge, Cradlebough, who had himself visited Mountain Meadows eighteen months after the massacre, while the skeletons of the emigrants were still lying there, delivered an outstanding opening address to the jury members, as has already been cited, concerning the need of punishing the numerous criminals of the period of terror, unless the entire people [of Utah]* were to be regarded as responsible and liable to punishment. But the grand jury, which consisted of Mormons, accomplished absolutely nothing in the case, even though an overwhelming abundance of evidence was brought in.

*These
words add-
ed for clar-
ity.—Trans.

Cradlebough, who left Utah some time afterward, then appealed to the Congress of the United States and presented to them in eloquent terms the details of the massacre, according to the testimonies which he had brought to light. Incidentally, since these substantially concur with the "Argus" letter, we shall cite here only a couple of these statements. The Mormons laid the entire blame on the Indians, and in regard to that he said:

> During our stay in Santa Clara I received a visit from some Indian chiefs, who gave me their account of the massacre. They admitted that some of their men had taken part in it, but no Indians were present at the assault. A chief named Jackson stated in the presence of others that a white man came to their camp the day before the attack, with a piece of paper which he said that Brigham Young had sent, which ordered them to go up and help in the slaughter of the emigrants. Some of the tribe went there, but did not take part in the engagement, because the emigrants had long rifles and shot well. Jackson's brother was shot while he was running across the meadow about 200 yards away from the emigrants' firing line.
>
> [p. 166] Jackson said that all the Mormons were painted; and further, that the Indians received a portion of the pieces of clothing; and that the most important leaders were John D. Lee, President Haight, and Bishop Heigbee [sic]. Later another Indian showed me the spot, he said, where the Mormons had disguised and painted themselves. Here it should be observed that the Indians in Southern Utah are not very numerous, and have a rather low standing. They are cowardly and very primitive. Very few of them have guns. They are not dangerous; I hardly think that all the Indians in the southern part of Utah could manage to do battle with ten white men!

In regard to the surviving children of the emigrants, the Judge said:

> I remember one of them, a boy named John Calvin, just about ten years old, who one day after he had sat quietly and meditated for a while, exclaimed with these words: "Oh, if only I were big, I know what I would do then; I would shoot John D. Lee. I saw him shoot my mother!" I will never forget the look on that boy's face!

Mr. Jacob Forney, Brigham Young's successor as Indian Agent, gathered sixteen of these children together and sent them to St. Louis. In his report to the government he gave the children's names[c] and passed on many serious matters in regard to the Mormons.

[p. 167] In March 1859 he wrote as follows: "I am in a position to show that property in the amount of about $30,000 was distributed among the leading church officials a few days after the massacre."

In September of the same year it states in his report:

> I began my investigations without prejudice, in the hope of being in a position to lay the blame for the whole offense upon the Indians. But unfortunately everything has convinced me that they were merely playing the role of assistants. . . . White men were present and they led the Indians. John D. Lee told me in his own home last April in the presence of two men, that he was present in the engagement for three days, among which was the final day. . . .

It is highly regrettable that the government in Washington, notwithstanding such an abundance of information made known in connection with the case, has taken no steps to have the perpetrators punished.

This word added for clarity.
—Trans.

c. This report goes as follows: John Calvin, 8 years old, does not remember his [family]* name, but says that his parents lived in Horse Head, Johnston County, Arkansas. Mironi, seven years old, and William Taggit, four years old, are brothers, also from Johnston County. Prudence Angeline, six years old, and Anna, about three; these two were assumed to be sisters. Rebecca, nine years old, Louise, five years old, and Sarah, three years old, are from Dunlap. Betsey, six years old, Anna, three years old, are thought to be sisters, and nothing is known of their family or home town. Charles Francher, eight, and his sister Anna, three. Saphronia or Marie Huff, six, and Elizabeth Huff, four years old. A boy without a description; the people he lived with called him William. Francis Hawn or Korn, four years old. After conversations with these children I have come to the conclusion that most of them are from Johnston County, Arkansas. Most of them have told me that their grandparents live in that state. Mr. Hamlin has grounds for believing that a boy about eight years old and from the same group is now with the Navajo Indians near the Colorado River. In regard to these unhappy children Forney relates further in his report to the Commission on Indian Affairs, dated Provo City, March 1859: "The children were sold off to various people in Cedar City and Pinto Creek. I am now in possession of bills from various persons who are requesting payment from the government, but I cannot bring myself even to present demands of this sort to the Department." At the last session of the US Congress an attempt was made to award these bereaved children a few hundred acres of government land by way of compensation for the loss which they must have sustained from the murder of their parents and guardians. But even this met with opposition from the generous-minded statesmen, for they feared that such nobleminded action would set a dangerous example for others who might suffer in similar manner.

When a petition to this effect was once introduced into Congress, one member asked: "Has murder been committed in Utah during the last twenty years?"

"Yes," came the answer.

"In the last fifteen yeears?"

"Yes."

"In the last ten years?"

"Yes."

"In the last five years?"

"Perhaps not." [p. 168]

"Good! If there has been no murder in Utah for five years, then I am opposed to reviving the distant past. There are murders in New York almost every day!" Such a mode of treatment and such pronouncements as this presumably need no further comment!

In July 1875 Judge Boreman for the first time brought one of the culprits, the aforementioned John D. Lee, into court in Beaver City, Utah. After encountering many difficulties he also secured witnesses, among whom were two eyewitnesses: namely, Joel White and the previously mentioned Bishop Klingonsmith—who, all things considered, can be regarded as the most important witness that had yet come forward.[d]

His statement is not quoted here, however, since it substantially agrees completely with the presentation in "Argus." Before the trial began, John D. Lee meanwhile tried to appear as the public prosecutor in order to free himself.

---

d. During the hearing Judge Sutherland, one of the attorneys for the Church and the defense attorney for Lee, put to Klingonsmith the following probing question, with the thought that since the witness was an accomplice and already sixty-three years old, he would not confess his own crime: "I presume," said the clever attorney, "that you fired your gun over the heads of the emigrants?" The answer was, "I fired right at them, and I presume I hit my man." Bishop Klingonsmith, who must have been driven by the prick of conscience, was removed or chased out of Utah to the neighboring state of Nevada, where in the District Court, April 10, 1871, he submitted a written and sworn confession which in every detail agreed with the oral testimony which he had given at the local hearing [in Utah].* *These words added for clarity.—Trans.* His written testimony concluded as follows: "I began to collect the children even before the shooting had ceased. I have submitted this testimony before the present court (in Nevada), because I believe that I would be murdered if I tried to present the same before any court in the Territory of Utah." He also confirms the fact there that Brigham Young had the supreme command (as "Commander in Chief") over the troops who perpetrated the massacre, and that John D. Lee submitted a full report concerning it to President Young as "Commander in Chief."

And the court accepted his proposal in the hope that it might thereby clarify Brigham Young's true relationship to the massacre.

[p. 169] Consequently Lee worked out a kind of "confession," but in it he exonerated Brigham Young from all involvement. It went as follows:

> . . . I must say to Brigham Young's credit that he wept like a baby and wrung his hands in bitter torment of soul when he heard my report of the massacre. He said that it was the most unfortunate incident that had ever befallen the Mormons, and that this deed would bring sorrow and misfortune upon Utah. He wished that God had prevented its occurrence. . . .

In that case Brigham must have recovered himself remarkably soon, for shortly afterward he was dealing with the matter in Bishop Klingonsmith's presence in a very cold-blooded fashion. Bishop Klingonsmith, whose truthfulness must be regarded as removed from all doubt, relates the following:

> . . . The next day Lee, Charles Hopkins and I met in President Young's office. Brigham treated us in a friendly manner and took us over to his stable to show us his carriages, horses and other fine items. In the course of the conversation he said that I, who had supervision over the final effects of the emigrants, should turn them over to Lee, since he was the Indian Agent, and as such had the greatest right to distribute them. Then he turned to me and said, "Don't tell anyone what you know about this matter; don't even talk to each other about it. . . ."

Therefore the judge rejected Lee's confession[e] [p. 170] as useless, and the trial against him got under way. The defendants—among whom the salaried attorneys, Messrs. Sutherland and Bates occupied a prominent place—

---

e. From John D. Lee's confession we will further quote the following excerpt, which testifies clearly enough who was the prime mover of this inhuman slaughter: "It is my painful but unavoidable obligation to write down the circumstances which led to this unhappy affair called 'The Mountain Meadow Massacre'. . . . I had been arrested and arraigned for participation in the above-mentioned crime. I have now been in prison for more than eight months, shackled in irons for three of them. . . . I have endeavored to bear this with launched out as usual with laying the blame upon the Indians. The emigrants were supposed to have aroused the hatred of the savages by bringing poison into a spring and then leaving a dead, poisoned cow in their pathway of which the redskins later partook. We should not tarry over the illogical and fanciful elements in such stories as these, but let us just for a moment dream up the possibility that the redskins perpetrated the murder, notwithstanding the clearest, most irrefutable evidence to the contrary adduced by the opposing side. Then we ask the very simple questions: "Why didn't the 400-man Nauvoo Legion, which no one denies was present, prevent the massacre? It would have been easy for them to do so. Why didn't the Mormons help the emigrants against the savages?" Is not neutrality under such circumstances the same thing as complicity in guilt? But it does no good to do any arguing so long as every jury in Utah according to US law is to consist of Mormons—since Mormons are obliged by secret oath to acquit their brethren in the faith who are accused in the courts of the "heathen." In the trial of Mr. Lee the jury consisted of eight Mormons and four "heathen." The outcome was consequently that they could not agree [on a verdict],* and the complaint against Lee had to be put to rest.

If the US government does not soon get to work on the case, the "hounds of Mountain Meadows" will remain unpunished until their dying day, and the blood of their murdered victims will ever continue to cry out to heaven for vengeance.*

*These words added for clarity.—Ed.

*It is possible that this booklet was rushed to completion before it was finished off with a proper concluding chapter, in order to present it at the time of a renewed trial of Lee and his accomplices in the massacre. That would account for its rather abrupt ending. There is, however, another possibility: that the final pages of the work have been removed or inadvertently lost. —Trans.

---

fortitude, knowing that most of those who took part in this unhappy affair were motivated by religious influence or fanaticism; and nothing else but commitment to God and their duty to Him as taught to them in their religion and by the leaders of their church could ever have prevailed upon them to perpetrate these abhorrent and unnatural deeds. I am convinced that all or most of those who took part in this lamentable affair did so on the basis of obedience to their orders which they regarded as their duty—their religious duty—to obey." (Cf. "John D. Lee's Hearing," July 1875, p. 10.)

Moody Press, a ministry of the Moody Bible Institute, is designed for education, evangelization, and edification. If we may assist you in knowing more about Christ and the Christian life, please write us without obligation: Moody Press, c/o MLM, Chicago, Illinois 60610.